Getting a Life

To Beth,

who knows what love is,

and has a life.

Getting a Life

Strategies for Joyful
&
Effective Living

Copthorne Macdonald

HOUNSLOW

Getting a Life: Strategies for Joyful & Effective Living

Hounslow Press
A member of the Dundurn Group

Publisher: Anthony Hawke
Editor: Nadine Stoikoff
Designer: Andy Tong
Printer: Webcom

Canadian Cataloguing in Publication Data

Macdonald, Copthorne
    Getting a life : strategies for joyful & effective living

Includes bibliographical references.
ISBN 0-88882-178-6

1. Conduct of life. 2. Success. 3. Happiness.
I. Title.

BF637. C5M3 1995   158   C95-931122-X

Publication was assisted by the Canada Council, the Book Publishing Industry Development Program of the Department of Canadian Heritage, the Ontario Arts Council, and the Ontario Publishing Centre of the Ministry of Citizenship, Culture, and Recreation.

Acknowledgements

The "Being-Values" from Abraham Maslow, TOWARD A PSYCHOLOGY OF BEING, Second Edition, Van Nostrand Reinhold, New York, NY, are reprinted by permission.

Brief quotations from ZEN AND THE ART OF MOTORCYCLE MAINTENANCE, by Robert M. Pirsig. Text: Copyright © 1974 by Robert M. Pirsig. By permission of William Morrow & Company, Inc.

Brief quotations from BLACKBERRY WINTER, by Margaret Mead. Text: Copyright © 1972 by Margaret Mead. By permission of William Morrow & Company, Inc.

The Lewis Thomas quote is from his article "Note from a Universe Watcher: 'We are the Newest, the Youngest, and the Brightest Thing Around'" that appeared in the New York Times of July 2, 1978. Copyright © 1978 By the New York Times Company. Reprinted by permission.

The Gail Sheehy quote is from PASSAGES by Gail Sheehy. Copyright © 1974, 1976 by Gail Sheehy. Used by permission of Dutton Signet, a division of Penguin Books USA Inc.

Printed and bound in Canada

Hounslow Press
2181 Queen Street East
Suite 301
Toronto, Ontario, Canada
M4E 1E5

Hounslow Press
73 Lime Walk
Headington, Oxford
England
OX3 7AD

Hounslow Press
1823 Maryland Avenue
P.O. Box 1000
Niagara Falls, NY
U.S.A. 14302-1000

Contents

Acknowledgements

A few years ago Jim Cody, a journalist friend of mine, commented that I had some worthwhile things to say about dealing with everyday life situations. Jim suggested that I write a book that dealt with practical, everyday *applied wisdom*. *Getting a Life* is that book, and I greatly appreciate Jim's suggestion.

I also appreciate the encouragement, support, and helpful suggestions received from many other people during the writing and refining of the book. Special thanks to my brother David Macdonald who you will meet in chapter 4, and to my brother Dan Macdonald whose encouragement about the merits of the project was much appreciated.

Discussions with Beverly Mills Stetson, Virginia Kouyoumdjian, Deirdre Kessler, John DeGrace, and my late friend T. Thacher Robinson left their mark on this book. So did the much-appreciated feedback from David Stetson, Martin Rutte, Maida Rogerson, and Scott Rathjen. Naturally, as I go back in time the list of contributors grows impossibly long. To these many unnamed people who influenced me in positive ways — and thus helped this book come to fruition — sincere thanks.

Introduction

This book is about crafting full, rich, creative, and enjoyable lives for ourselves — lives that are significant, lives that contribute in some way to the world around us. *Getting a Life* is rooted in the idea that some steps toward wisdom require nothing more than a fresh look at common life situations, nothing more than an appreciation of the difference between skilful and unskilful ways of dealing with those situations. Its premise is that a few truths about everyday life, if pointed out and taken seriously, can make a significant difference in the quality of day-to-day living and our enjoyment of life.

Getting a Life is also a book about applied, practical wisdom. Aristotle differentiated between two aspects of wisdom — one addressing existential and metaphysical issues, the other addressing everyday life. The poet Coleridge called this second *practical* variety of wisdom "Common sense in an uncommon degree."

An earlier book of mine, *Toward Wisdom: Finding Our Way to Inner Peace, Love & Happiness* dealt mostly with the meaning-of-life kind of wisdom — the big-picture, existential kind. It is this aspect of wisdom that spiritual paths help us develop if we are willing to make the necessary (and often considerable) commitment of time and effort. Practical wisdom, on the other hand, is much more accessible.

Although wisdom has not been discussed much during the past fifty years, most of us do have some rough, fuzzy sense of what the word means. For many people wisdom simply means lots of knowledge. But wisdom is more than that. While there is not yet one sharp, clear definition of wisdom that everyone agrees upon, efforts are being made to bring the concept back into common use and to refine our understanding of it. Academic researchers and others are investigating wisdom and are attempting to get a clear picture of its constituents.

I don't have a final, complete understanding either, but I'd like to share with you my present sense of the nature of wisdom. In my view, wisdom comprises certain extraordinary

- *attitudes,*
- value-based *ways of being,* and
- perspectives and interpretive frameworks that we might call *ways of seeing.*

Each item on the list that follows strikes me as an element of practical wisdom in the sense that each makes a real, useful, *practical* contribution to the life of the wise person. Also, some constituents of wisdom that were only of philosophical interest in Aristotle's time are today of extreme practical importance. For instance, our world is currently experiencing negative impacts from billions of technology-equipped, self-interested people, and these impacts threaten the long-term viability of the biosphere. Being able to see interconnectedness and appreciate oneness (characteristics listed below) might well be essential for preserving that viability.

WISE ATTITUDES:
- feeling fully responsible for one's life choices and actions
- a positive "let's make the most of it" attitude
- a reality-seeking, truth-seeking orientation
- a desire to learn, and a feeling of responsibility for one's own learning
- a desire to grow, to develop, "to become all I am capable of becoming"

WISE WAYS OF BEING:
- being attentive: aware of mind events and processes as well as what is happening in our immediate situation
- being creative: producing uniqueness and novelty that has value
- cooperative functioning of intellect and intuition
- being self-disciplined: able to work now for a reward later
- being courageous: able to face dangers and fears with clarity and skill

- being aware of one's own eventual death to the degree that it helps guide one's life
- dealing with situations appropriately, using a large repertoire of approaches and techniques. Being able to choose the approach that best fits each situation: appropriate planning, appropriate timing, appropriate problem-solving, dealing with commitments appropriately, etc.
- being non-reactive: able to deal skilfully with powerful emotions
- being deeply loving, and able to manifest love in appropriate ways
- having a sense of wonder
- being compassionate
- behaving in ways that benefit others
- deeply valuing wholeness, perfection, completion, justice, aliveness, richness, simplicity, beauty, goodness, uniqueness, effortlessness, playfulness, truth, honesty, reality, self-sufficiency (Psychologist Abraham Maslow's *Being-Values*)[1]

WISE WAYS OF SEEING:

- clear comprehension of "the laws of life": deeply understanding *causes* and *consequences* in interpersonal, societal, employment, and other arenas
- seeing happiness and joy as unconditional and always available
- self-knowledge and a realistic self-concept
- appreciation of the enduring *structural* and moment-to-moment *content* aspects of life, and their relationship to each other
- holistic seeing: an appreciation of system, interconnectedness, oneness, the evolutionary process, and the complex nature of causation
- recognition that there are limits to personal knowledge and there may well be limits to the ability of our species to know

Wisdom is not an absolute. Not all of these qualities need be present to an equal degree in each wise person. But in any person worthy of being called *wise*, many of them will be present and relatively well developed. Often, wise people will have developed a few of these qualities to an exceptional degree.

The particular qualities developed will differ from person to person, and this results in each wise person's wisdom having a distinct character or "flavour."

The world is not divided into wise and unwise people. None of us is perfectly wise or totally unwise. As I see it, each of us is wise to the extent that the characteristics just listed are part of us, to the extent that we actually live them. If we want to become wiser people, we need to further develop these characteristics and incorporate them into our lives. Fortunately, the acquisition of wisdom is not something that we must leave to the whims of fate, as many in the past have assumed. Wisdom can be developed intentionally. Wisdom can be learned. Living skilfully helps us develop greater wisdom, and greater wisdom helps us live more skilfully. The two are intimately entwined.

Getting a Life attempts to reinforce our best intuitions and intentions, lead us to some fresh insights about everyday life, and help us develop that *uncommon degree of common sense.* The first sixteen chapters focus on the life-building process and on various challenges associated with daily living. They discuss skilful and not-so-skilful ways of dealing with these challenges. In the process, we are introduced to some wiser-than-usual ways of looking at the situation — to some perspectives that promise to change our lives for the better. The final five chapters deal with ways of developing wise responses and attitudes toward life happenings, plus some wise ways of seeing and interpreting the data of life. The aim of this final part of the book is to guide us toward those all-win mind spaces that are enjoyable to experience, good for us, and indirectly benefit others.

Enjoy!

1

Getting a Life

On a recent book tour I was guest-of-the-day on an open-line radio show. The show's host was a feisty, thirtyish young woman who obviously cared about people. Listeners called in with various concerns about personal growth and wisdom, and she and I did our best to respond. Then a man in his late twenties called. He let us know that he was bored and tired. Nothing engaged his interest, he reported, and very little ever seemed to go right in his life. I responded as supportively as I knew how, and suggested several things that he might do to stir up a little zest for living. No luck; the caller found fault with every suggestion. Finally, the program's host — exasperated with both the caller's self-pitying attitude and my over-solicitous approach — took over the discussion. She was direct. Totally up-front with her frustration, she told him to "stop making excuses and *Get a life!*" He and he alone was responsible for putting his life in shape.

What is involved in getting a life? How do we move from apathy or a blame-others, self-pitying mindset to full responsibility for running our lives? Joseph Campbell knew the answer. He advised his students at Sarah Lawrence College to *follow their bliss*. What did he mean by that? He meant build your life on what excites you and draws you to it; find and follow some activity that engages your interest and imagination and creativity.

I recently spoke to a group of graduating high school students. I told them that I was sure that their parents and other relatives were all excited that graduation was here, but I was also sure that many of the students themselves were not. I put the following chart on the blackboard, and asked each person to locate the spot on the chart that corresponded to the mental state they experience when thinking about their near-term future.

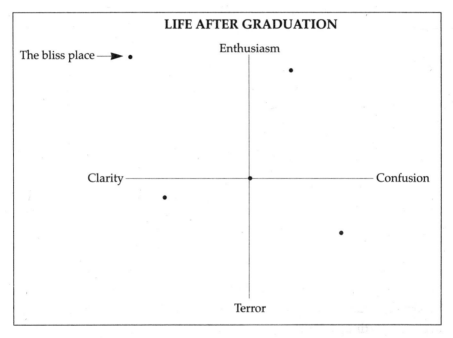

The first student to share her state of mind with the rest of us picked the spot I have marked as *The bliss place*: maximum clarity and maximum enthusiasm. Another student picked the intersection of the two lines — not high clarity, nor total confusion, and neither enthusiastic nor terrified — a "life goes on" sort of mindspace. No one admitted being totally confused and terrified, but some responses were in that direction.

As our lives unfold we find ourselves all over this chart. Even those who manage to find their bliss, their flow, their first-choice of a life engagement, may meet circumstances along the way that separate them from it. That's life. Things happen that severely rock the boat. Yet there exists, always, the possibility of re-entering that mental state of bliss, or flow, or high clarity and enthusiasm. Doing that is made immensely easier if we have created an appropriate life structure; if we have done the right sort of assessing and experimenting. In any case, when we find ourselves floundering around elsewhere on the chart, we can use the bliss place as a beacon. We can let it reassure us when we are on course, and pull us toward it when we are not.

As I see it, creating a life for oneself involves four things:

- becoming clear about the values that we would like our life to embody and promote
- assessing our talents and skills
- setting appropriate life goals, and devising strategies for reaching them, and
- seeing how the resulting life stands up to one or more objective standards

Let's look at these one by one.

What is worth doing? What kind of life do I want to lead? In what sort of doing am I apt to find my creative opportunity, my flow, my bliss? It all starts with our values, and becoming clear about what is truly important to us. Once that's clear, the details will follow. Robert Pirsig called value "the leading edge of reality" and noted that "value is the predecessor of structure." We need to ask: "What is deeply meaningful to me? What matters to me enough to devote the energy and time of my life to it?" Only if I consciously come to terms with those questions can I be sure that the life I create is one that will resonate with deep meaning for me — a life that I can be completely satisfied with, and proud of.

The answer may be deceptively simple. *Being a friend* is the central value in the life of one wise person I know. For someone else I admire it is *raising sane kids.* Other (often unexamined) values include *making a living, having fun,* and *becoming rich and famous.* For an increasing number of people their own growth and development is a motivating value — the desire to *become all I am capable of becoming.*

The great task of my parents' and grandparents' era was that of building North America — creating the infrastructure of public works, manufacturing plants, and businesses that allow you and me to live more comfortably than prior generations did. Our parents and grandparents succeeded in what they set out to do. North America has been developed — perhaps even over-developed. Now, you and I live in a different historical moment. Other tasks and other duties call to my generation, and that of my daughter and granddaughters.

What are the principles upon which we want to base our lives and our livelihood? Do we follow a livelihood that contributes to present problems, or do we turn to one that contributes to their solution? Are we willing to avoid involvement with what demeans and tears down, even if doing that means changing our lives and perhaps making some sacrifices? Can we actualize higher values such as resolving conflicts, creating beauty, helping others find truth and wisdom?

Once we have played around in the non-specific realm of values for a while, and some sense of purpose and general direction has begun to form, the next step is to assess our capabilities. What skills have I already developed? And what talents do I have that I might develop further? In short, what do I appear capable of doing now and in the long run? For many, identifying the route to the place of bliss requires only this kind of reflection. For others, it involves serious (and sometimes prolonged) investigative work.

In thinking about our capabilities and potentials it's important to consider all of them. The recent work of Harvard psychologist Howard Gardner has clarified the nature of intelligence. Gardner says that we have seven kinds of intelligence, and that IQ tests measure only two of them: *Linguistic Intelligence*, and *Logical-Mathematical Intelligence*. The other five are

- *musical intelligence,*
- *spatial intelligence* (the kind that artists, architects, and mechanical engineers have lots of),
- *bodily-kinesthetic Intelligence* (possessed in abundance by athletes, dancers, and brain surgeons),
- *interpersonal intelligence* (the ability to understand other people), and
- *interpersonal intelligence* (the ability to know oneself).

Thomas Armstrong's book, *7 Kinds of Smart,* is a useful guide to Gardner's ideas, and is designed to help readers explore their own strengths and weaknesses among the seven.

The schooling process, from grade 1 through university, rewards people who are skilled at logic, mathematics, and manipulating words. And despite protests to the contrary, many schools give people who are not particularly good at these things the message that they are less valuable, less worthy people than those who are good at them. Gardner, on the other hand, shows us a broader field of competencies. Failure to excel at two of the seven says nothing about our potential in the other five areas. Might not our capabilities in one of these other areas be something upon which to build a life?

As a young person I found my bliss in radio and electronics, and I followed this bliss right into engineering school. Yet that bliss evaporated the very first day. The head of the Electrical Engineering Department gave an introductory lecture to all us new students. At one point in his talk he made a dreadful pronouncement: "If you don't love mathematics you will never make it through engineering school."

I was terrified. I loved electronics but not math. Math had never been one of my strengths, and I came rather close to hating it. In the end, the head of the Department turned out to be wrong. My love of electronics, my central bliss, was strong enough to get me to buckle down, dig into this distasteful stuff, and learn what I needed to learn to get through engineering school. I never did come to love math, but I learned enough of it to graduate, and afterward to follow my bliss in electronic design work.

My point is this: becoming involved in an activity that has meaning and emotional juice — and perhaps even excelling at it — does not mean that we have to excel at every sub-skill. We just have to be passably good at those skills. Very often, time, effort, and an average mind prove to be a perfectly adequate substitute for inborn brilliance. How many young women with superb interpersonal skills and the potential to become brilliant counsellors and therapists have been scared away from university-level psychology programs because they needed to take a statistics course? It's sad. Let your bliss arouse you and motivate you to do the dog work that keeps the bliss alive and opens new doors.

Once we have at least a hint of where our bliss might lie, some clarity about values, and some sense of our present and potential capabilities, it's time to consider specific goals, and to select one or more as our own. How we frame a goal can make a difference. For example, becoming a famous rock musician has become the central goal of many young men. Yet *become a rock star* is too fuzzy a goal to be of much help in guiding an aspiring musician.

To get serious about this, the would-be musician needs to get more specific, more process oriented. Perhaps the important question is, "What are the key abilities which rock stars have that I need to develop?" Beneath all the fluff, style, and hype, it seems to me that the top stars have three abilities: they are superb instrumentalists, they can sing reasonably well, and they write their own material. So the original rather fuzzy goal really involves three concrete, process-related sub-goals: become an expert instrumentalist; learn to sing; and learn to write powerful music and lyrics.

Next, we need to select some long-term strategies and short-term compromises that seem likely to enable us to reach those goals. We need to assess the practical nitty-gritty stuff — the ways and the means — and then come up with some sort of tentative plan for getting started. Our aspiring rock musician might start by asking: How can I arrange my life to eat and pay the rent and still have time to develop my musical abilities? What aspect of my musical education do I work on first? Or do I work on all three simultaneously? Where do I find the guidance I need? Do I enrol in a school music program? Or do I find a musician who is willing to teach me? And what about forming a band with other beginning musicians?

I understand that Benjamin Franklin at age twenty made a plan for his entire life and continued to follow it on through old age. I am not suggesting that we do anything like this. I'm much more in tune with the idea of living day-to-day and moment-to-moment in response to the promptings of the wisdom within. But moment-to-moment living happens within a context, and it is by envisioning a future, setting goals, and making plans at appropriate points along the way that we choose what that context will be. If Mother Theresa had gone into accounting rather than becoming a nun, her life would have been very different. Certain opportunities for self-actualization would have been denied her, and certain others would have opened up.

Whether we attempt to plan it or just let it happen, each life develops a contextual framework. That structure of goals, work, relationships, and learning activities determines much of what can and cannot happen within that life. My point is that forethought about this contextual framework beats the hell out of just letting it happen. Of course, live moment-by-moment. But do it within a context that you find exciting and fulfilling.

My own experience also indicates that during the process of setting goals and selecting strategies it helps to get specific about time. About ten years after starting my engineering career I began to think about a career change. I said to myself, "In the long run, I'm going to write," but I didn't get specific about when. It was ten years later before I finally told myself: "The long run is here!" and began working on a book. Yet things still moved slowly. Eight more years passed before I began writing full time, and another eight before my first close-to-the-heart book was published. That's twenty-six years total! It's clear to me now that this new career would have taken off much more quickly if I had

- set more-specific goals for myself,
- linked goals to specific dates and periods of time, and
- given more thought to ways, means, and strategies.

I'm not suggesting that we should establish cast-in-stone time lines, but I am suggesting that we think through a five-year- or two-year- or seven-year plan that makes present sense. And then change or abandon it as the reality of our life unfolds.

Related to creating a plan is the idea of running life experiments. If the activity under consideration has some appeal, but we're not sure that it should become a major focus of attention and energy, then the most sensible thing is to run a time-limited, resources-limited experiment of some kind. We try. We test. We find out. The idea is to get deeply enough involved to know if the activity is capable of transporting us into that mental space of enthusiasm, and high clarity that *this is it*. Naturally, the how, what, where, and when of each experiment will be different, and setting one up is often a creative challenge.

Finally, we ask ourselves, "How does this life I have imagined for myself compare with various yardsticks of successful living proposed by myself and others?" In choosing values on which to base my life I have also chosen the way I will measure the success of that life. When I compare the actual living and doing with the values my life seeks to emulate and actualize, is it a success? Or perhaps I'm just in the process of planning a life. In that case, are the specific goals and strategies that I've decided upon in harmony with those values, and are they likely to make things happen in accord with those values?

Many other standards have been proposed, and it might be instructive to compare the intended life with a few of them. Three that I have found helpful I call *The Existentialists' Test*, *The Saints' Test*, and *The Universe's Test*.

The existentialists — Sartre, Camus, and others — rejected the handed-down-from-heaven moral codes of organized religion, and said, instead, that humanity must define itself, its purposes, and its own rules of behaviour. The Existentialists held that human nature is not something determined in advance which our lives merely reflect. Rather, human actions come first. Human nature, to the existentialist, is an after-the-fact concept determined by what people actually do — by their behaviour, by the lives that they live. You, and I, and everyone else define what it means to be human by the choices we make, by the way we live our lives. In the Existentialists' view, good intentions don't count; what counts is what we actually do, how we actually live. Thus, *The Existentialists' Test* involves asking ourselves questions like: What are the lasting effects of the life I have chosen to live? What is its significance in the larger scheme of things? Am I happy with the way that my life defines human nature?

If spirituality is central to one's life plan, then it seems appropriate to bring out that cluster of qualities I call *The Saints' Test*. They include: living attentively, non-harmfulness, acceptance, courage, equanimity, and behaviour that benefits others.

Thinking about *behaviour that benefits others* carries me back to my university days. In the engineering lounge there was a frame on the wall into which, each week, a new card would appear that displayed some helpful saying or aphorism. One week the card carried a statement by the nineteenth-century Quaker, Étienne de Grellet:

> I shall pass through this world but once. If, therefore,
> there is any good thing I can do or any kindness I can
> show, let me do it now. Let me not defer it or neglect
> it, for I shall not pass this way again.

It made such sense to me. I copied it down, and carried it in my wallet for years. I can't imagine a better definition of everyday saintliness.

The outpost of universal process called Earth is going through rough times these days. Nature, by way of that group of activities we call evolution, has created wondrously complex and sophisticated systems here. Unfortunately, several billion systems of a type called the *human being* are behaving unwisely. They are, in fact, threatening the very continuation of the Earth Experiment. *The Universe's Test* involves putting ourselves in the position of the universal process itself, and asking whether this life — as I am living it — is helping the process or hindering it. Is my life

- helping to create a sustainable process?
- helping others to develop whole-process understanding — that more connections-oriented, complete, and long-term way of comprehending the reality around us?
- helping the universe to actualize its highest potential?

In summary, *Getting a Life* is no simple matter. The alternative, however, is to waste the precious opportunity we have to make the most of the one that the universe has given us.

2

Being a Learner

The process of crafting rewarding lives for ourselves calls for much learning, and it is important that we realize three things:

1. There are many learning options other than schools.
2. We must take personal responsibility for the learning process.
3. In this post-modern knowledge-based world we will need to spend our entire lives learning.

In recent years, things have become twisted around. Somehow the focus has shifted from the learning end of things (human curiosity, human need-to-know, and the appropriateness of self-directed exploration) to the teaching end of things (schools, teachers, and classrooms).

Learning is fundamental; teaching is secondary, incidental, instrumental. Teaching may help learning to happen, but so may a good night's sleep, being in an interesting place, and a thousand other things. Skilled teachers, and parents and friends can help us learn, but the learning itself is up to us. As teachers readily admit, if someone doesn't want to learn, teaching them won't cause much learning to take place. There will no doubt continue to be a place in our lives and in the lives of our children for schools of some sort, but learning is not just a time-limited, school-connected thing.

Learning is up to us. We are responsible for our own learning. As individuals, we must decide *that* we want to learn, *what* we want to learn, and take responsibility for making it happen. Many people emerge from their schooling never having learned that, and today find themselves in a terrible bind. The days are long gone when what you learned by age twenty or twenty-five would do you for the rest of your life. Rapid changes in world and workplace are rendering whole industries obsolete within breathtakingly short periods, and this pace of change seems destined to continue. Lifetime learning is here, and here to stay, and the fortunate ones will be those who are drawn to it with enthusiasm.

There are today, and always have been, people who saw the appropriateness of self-directed learning. It is not a new idea. A century ago it was championed by the Chautauqua movement. A few decades later the American philosopher and educator John Dewey promoted it. And since the 1960s, the resources available to self-directed learners have greatly increased, both in variety and quantity.

Concerning the education of children, there have always been parents who focused on learning rather than schooling. The education of anthropologist Margaret Mead is an example. Margaret grew up in a family that valued academic achievement. Her father was on the faculty of the Wharton School of Finance and Commerce at the University of Pennsylvania. Her mother was a graduate of the University of Chicago who later in life, after the demands of child rearing waned, went back to work on her Ph.D. Yet between kindergarten and high school Margaret spent only one year in school. The rest of the time she learned under the guidance of her grandmother who spent about an hour a day with her. As Margaret put it in her autobiography, *Blackberry Winter.*[2]

> I was not well drilled in geography or spelling. But I learned
> to observe the world around me and to note what I saw —
> to observe flowers and children and baby chicks. She taught
> me to read for the sense of what I read, and to enjoy learn-
> ing ... Looking back, my memories of learning precise skills,
> memorizing long stretches of poetry, and manipulating

paper are interwoven with memories of running — running in the wind, running through meadows, and running along country roads — picking flowers, running through meadows, hunting for nuts, and weaving together old stories and new events into myths about a rock or a tree.

It would be hard to find a better example of a lifelong learner than Margaret Mead. Her grandmother's approach obviously worked. It stimulated attentiveness, curiosity, and imagination — an orientation to life which helped Margaret Mead become one of this century's great anthropologists.

Whether the young people in our lives attend school or are home schooled, we parents and grandparents can help them get into the curious, excited, self-directed learning mode. And if they attend school, we can encourage the school to be responsive to their real needs. The turn-of-the century Russian Peter Kropotkin had some excellent advice for all us learners, young and old: "Find out what kind of world you want to live in, what you are good at, and what to work at to build that world. What do you need to know? Demand that your teachers teach you that."

Your childhood is over, and so is mine. Our schooling was whatever it was, and left its residue — some good, some bad. It failed to give us an ideal preparation for life, and now, no one is knocking on our doors offering to fill in the holes or repair the damage. It is up to each of us, as individuals, to do that. What are our options? What can we do to help ourselves and those we love to become enthusiastic life-long learners?

The starting point, as outlined in chapter 1, is some clarity about what kind of lives we want for ourselves — some sense of where we'd like to go with our lives, or at least a sense of what we want to explore or accomplish next. Once some degree of overall focus exists, it's time to get specific. What do the intentions you have about your life say about your next arena of action? And what skills do you need to develop to move into that arena? Are there any credentials that you need to acquire? Some sort of certification? What sort of learning strategy would allow you to accomplish what needs to be accomplished with an acceptable balance of time, money, and fun? Do you, for instance, take a Spanish course evenings at the local community college (low cost, little time, little fun)? Or do you spend three months in Cuernavaca, Mexico, attending classes at a local language institute (higher cost, more time, more fun)?

Exploring for resources is a highly individualized process. Our interests differ. And different people have different learning styles. For some, sitting in a classroom works — and feels right. For others it's immersing themselves in reading and following the path that opens up as each book or article leads to the next one. For still others it's an apprenticeship — learning by watching another person, and then trying the task ourself with that person looking over our shoulder and making suggestions.

One reason that self-directed learning is highly individualized is that learning resources are unevenly distributed. If one special person is your resource of choice, or one special educational institution, then you must be where that person or institution is. At the other extreme, if you are fortunate enough to learn readily from books and other print materials, or through on-line interaction at a computer screen and keyboard, geographical constraints may disappear entirely.

Information about the offerings of educational institutions is available in many communities. Check your local library for college catalogues and other descriptive material. And if the information you need is not there, your librarian can help you find addresses to write to for that information.

Tracking down non-institutional resources can be more of a challenge. Besides reading, what other kinds of self-directed learning options are there? Three popular ones are

- one-on-one mentoring and apprenticeship,
- learning through computer communication, and
- learning-oriented travel.

In times past it was common for would-be learners to seek out highly skilled people and arrange to learn from them. If it was a craft you wanted to learn, you apprenticed yourself to a master and worked under that person's influence and guidance. If you were academically inclined, you tried to become associated with an institution where the great minds in your field hung out.

Newly graduated Ph.D. scientists tried to get work in the labs of their scientific heroes. Perhaps I'm wrong, but it's my impression that many of us today have egos that are too big to be comfortable doing this sort of thing. Fewer people are willing to humble themselves enough to say: "I would like to learn from you." Yet the benefits of establishing a teacher/learner relationship with a highly talented person can be enormous.

If your proposed path of learning is in an unusual or specialized area, finding the right person to teach you could be a challenge in itself. One approach is to subscribe to magazines, journals, and newsletters that deal with the specialty. Read each issue carefully, and then follow up leads. Write to authors of articles, answer classified ads, or insert one of your own. Above all, don't hesitate to ask people for help in pointing you toward the kind of learning resources you're trying to find.

The Internet is one of two significant doors-to-learning that the computer has recently opened up. Because there are so many people on the Internet, so much information available, and so many groups devoted to specialized interests, Internet involvement presents the user with vast possibilities for interpersonal conversation, information exchange, and learning.

Much of the interaction and learning takes place in *Usenet News Groups,* and many Internet users find these groups a perfect place to meet knowledgeable people in their areas of interest. Each news group has a short Internet name and a defined topic area. You can join any group (or leave it) at your pleasure, and there are no costs beyond those associated with connecting to the Internet network itself. When you check into a news group you have the opportunity to read messages posted by members of that group, starting with those most recently posted. You can skip the messages you don't want to read, read the ones you do, and post your own messages for the rest of the group to read.

Especially if you are looking for esoteric information, posting a message can be very fruitful. Whatever your question is, it is very likely that within a few hours of posting your query, one or more people would have posted reply comments.

Other major Internet aids-to-learning include e-mail, "listserv" mailing lists, and electronic publications. News Group interactions frequently lead to friendships and to one-on-one exchanges of information by e-mail. The list-serv function allows whole groups to be served by e-mail. An e-mail message to a listserv address results in duplicate messages being sent to all members of that listserv group. Electronic publications are magazines or academic journals that are distributed to subscribers (usually at no cost) by e-mail.

The Internet is vast, complex, and constantly changing. That said, the Internet is also very easy to get involved with and explore. You don't have to have a whit of interest in computers, or any technical savvy at all. You just need a basic computer, a modem, and communications software — all of which can be set up for you by some computer-literate other person, perhaps the teenager next door. The exploring itself involves typing short commands on the computer keyboard — something that grade-schoolers soon get quite adept at. If you can hunt and peck type on a typewriter, you can cruise the Internet on a computer keyboard. With some software, it's even easier: you just "point and click."

A good way to get a sense of Internet resources that might be of interest is to browse through one of the many directories and guides available at book stores and public libraries. If what you see there twigs your interest, the next step is to track down a service that will give you and your computer access to the Internet. These differ greatly in the level of service offered and the cost to the user. Talk with computer-savvy people about the connection options available in your area.

Distance education or *distance learning* is the second computer-assisted door to learning. It's the latest wrinkle in home-study or extension education, but its adoption by some prestigious institutions lends weight to the possibility that we really do have something significant here, and not just a fad. In one ad, New York's venerable New School for Social Research says that they now offer "a new way to complete courses for academic credit or personal development without traveling to attend class. Using a computer and a modem, you can go to class at any time from work, from home, or on the road — just turn on your computer and be at The New School ..."[3]

Learning-oriented travel can take various forms. All travel helps us learn — even the most unplanned, unstructured, casual travel. Actually going there makes places come alive and people become real in ways that reading about them never could. On the other hand, well-prepared travelers do get more out of their travel experiences than poorly prepared ones. Some of my friends read extensively before they travel. In doing so they learn about "can't miss" places to visit as well as places they'd just as soon avoid. One of my friends is an architecture buff, and he reads up beforehand on every cathedral and other major building he plans to visit, and enjoys them all the more for having done that.

Some people combine travel and taking courses. Naturally, if you have the time and the money, you can simply arrange with a far-away educational institution to attend classes there for a single term or longer. More feasible for many people over age sixty are the short courses and low-cost accommodations offered through Elderhostel.[4] There are Elderhostel programs all over North America and in a few other places in the world. The quality of accommodations, food, and courses varies from situation to situation, and is somewhat difficult to assess from a distance, but hey, a bit of risk is part of the adventure, isn't it?

3

Deferring Satisfaction

A ready-made wonderful life is rarely just handed to us. It is something we work to create. It is something we painstakingly build, element by element. Some of these efforts extend over long periods of time. And because of this, an important skill that we need to develop is the ability to work now, and for a sustained period, even though the reward will be a long time in coming. How do we develop this ability?

For me it all began one autumn day when I was nine years old. My mother, in a casual voice, asked, "Coppie, if you were going to play a musical instrument, what kind of instrument would you want to play?"

I didn't really know, but I remembered that Jimmy, the kid who used to live next door, had played the clarinet. "The clarinet," I said, and went back to my fun.

Christmas morning the consequences of my casual reply became apparent, and a great weight descended. Under the tree, on *my* side, was a shiny metal clarinet. The instant I saw it I felt horribly trapped. This was an extravagant gift that my parents couldn't really afford, and now they expected me to learn to play it.

My body and mind were soon engaged in music lessons and half-hour practice sessions, but my heart wasn't. I had no gift for the whole business, and no enthusiasm. Despite that, my playing slowly improved. Eventually, moments of fun and feelings of accomplishment began to arise from this musical drudgery. Although I never became a highly skilled clarinet player, I did get into the school orchestra and band, and that was fun. Marching band in high school was the most fun — trips away, being on the field during half time at the big game, all that. I began to be glad that I had developed at least some skill at this — enough skill, anyway, to open the door to these new kinds of fun.

This was my first experience with long-deferred satisfaction, my first experience at working hard now, with little immediate pleasure, to gain something worthwhile way down the road. At age nine I had absolutely no faith that anything good would ever come out of music lessons and practice — and I had no self-discipline to speak of, no way to keep myself at it. I kept at it because of the *external* discipline imposed on me by parents, music teacher, and the daily practice sessions.

Looking back, I see now that learning to play the clarinet was the least important thing I got out of this experience. The thing of lasting importance was coming to understand in a direct, personal way that **sometimes the pay-off comes only after a long period of hard, unrewarding work.** I suspect that this is one of those things you truly believe only after you experience it for yourself. Once developed, however, this belief emboldens us to try other long-term experiments, and perhaps even an occasional great adventure.

One way we can help our children develop self-discipline is to provide them with tools for exploration, and enough structure to keep them at it for a while. It might not be music, of course; it might be skiing, programing computers, getting a ham radio licence, learning to type, or a hundred other things.

"But kids' interests are so transient," you say.

Yes, they often are. Still, it is sometimes possible to sift out the winning interests from the rest before putting out really big bucks. Conditional support is one approach: sharing the burden, and getting some level of commitment from the child. If the interest is skiing, the parent might propose something like: "You want to learn to ski? Terrific. It's going to take money to start, and a lot of hard work to get good at it. I'll make you a deal. If you save up for the equipment and agree to take a lesson each time you go skiing, I'll pay for a winter's worth of lessons and lift tickets."

An extended period of hard work followed by some sort of significant payoff is what we're talking about here. If a person experiences that, then self-confidence soars and the foundations of *self*-discipline become established. Where parents are involved, they can sometimes structure the situation in ways that maximizes the chance of that happening. If the process does not reach the payoff stage the opposite could happen, so it's important to help a youngster select a first-time, long-term project that has a reasonable likelihood of success.

In situations having much externally applied structure, situations where one's nose is held to the grindstone by someone else, motivation may not matter much. Talent or no talent, motivation or no motivation, almost anyone who takes music lessons for three years and practises for half an hour a day will develop enough musical skill to play in school musical organizations. And almost anyone who takes a year-long, high school typing course will know how to touch type when that year is over. Sustained motivation becomes important when this kind of external structure is *not* there.

When there is little or no external structure to prod, guide, channel, or force us to continue, what does it take to carry us through to the end of a long-term project? *Sustained motivation* is one of those things. If every day we wake up enthusiastic about the project and are eager to get on with it, there is no problem. But our motivation rarely stays at a high level. We usually go through periods of diminished interest, diverted attention, and interfering priorities. When motivation wanes we must fall back on a belief that despite the draggy quality of the present, continued effort will eventually bring results.

This is where that magic something called *self-discipline* comes in. Self-discipline means going ahead even when enthusiasm wanes, even when the result seems distant, even when doubts arise about whether the result is worth the effort. Self-discipline involves visualizing the goal and turning repeatedly to that end-point vision — keeping it real and tangible and out in front throughout the project.

Self-discipline also involves seeing clearly that there is no evasive tactic that will get us to our goal. That procrastination won't work. That it is only by putting in the necessary hours of effort that we will eventually reach our goal.

Finally, self-discipline involves maintaining confidence that we are up to the task. This need not be an absolute confidence that we can reach the goal. It's more a perception that the likelihood of success is compatible with the level of effort. And where does this magic self-discipline stuff come from? I strongly suspect that it comes from having discovered for ourselves, at least once in our lives, that sustained effort with no immediate reward *really can* lead to important rewards later.

Having said all that, it sometimes makes sense to abandon a project. Perhaps, in the beginning, we underestimated the difficulty of the task or overestimated our ability. Perhaps some unanticipated "fatal flaw" appears along the way. In such cases dropping the project and moving on to something else may be the most sensible thing to do.

It is important when we abandon a project to avoid the temptation to slip into the I-have-failed mindset. Each of us is an experiment of nature, and each of us chooses an additional series of experiments that together constitute our life. Simply continuing to survive is a great accomplishment, and for most people, during most of human history, simply surviving absorbed all their time and energy. For many people that is still the case. If you have the luxury of extra time and extra energy to devote to activities beyond pure survival, does it make sense to waste that bounty on blue funks about things that failed to work out as you'd hoped? Grieve a bit, if need be, and then pour that excess energy into the *next* experiment.

We can take a lesson from toddlers. They reject the whole idea of failure. Life for them is one series of joyous experiments. They simply keep trying stuff. Sometimes they get it right and sometimes they don't. If it's important, they keep trying, and most of the time they eventually do get it right. If they conclude that the task really is impossible, they feel frustrated and disappointed and perhaps cry for a while — and then turn their attention to some other fun thing to do.

Perhaps you were one of those deprived kids who weren't forced to take music lessons, and now would like to raise your self-discipline level. Take heart. It's never too late to learn to play an instrument, and if music isn't your thing, there is probably some other set of skills you've always hankered for. Sign up, submit yourself to a big dose of externally applied discipline, and go through with it. Do it to get over that "Oh, I could never do that" feeling. Do it to expand your own sense of personal capability. Do it to convince yourself that long-term projects really can reach successful conclusions if you just keep making the effort.

4

Doing Things Carefully

My brother Dave has the attitude. I first noticed it twenty years ago when he showed me the boat he'd built. What a beauty! Every piece of hand-shaped wood was just right, and he'd given the boat many coats of spar varnish. This brought out the richness of the wood's grain and colour to the point where it almost glowed. Then there were those zillions of gigantic tomatoes that Dave grew on just three tomato plants; much care and attention to detail there, too. Now I see it in almost everything Dave does. It's even there in vacuuming the living room carpet and doing the dishes.

I once got a chance to watch him handle dishwashing away from his home turf. We'd had a big family meal, and Dave and I had volunteered to do the dishes. Dave was to wash; I was to dry.

I watched him size up the situation. I imagined him saying to himself, "No, there's no double sink here, and no dishpan ... rinsing will be a bit of a problem. Not much counter space on the left, but a good dish drainer ... it'll be okay if Cop dries fast enough. Hmmm, not much counter space on the right either ... ah, but with the dirty dishes stacked over on the table I can move a stack or two at a time."

There were great piles of dishes to deal with, and good conversation had already started to filter in from the living room. There was every reason to approach the task with minimal attention and a get-it-done-quick attitude, but this wasn't Dave's style. In the end, things did move quickly, but with much attention to detail, too. After half filling the sink and adding detergent, Dave began washing. His eyes seemed to hang on each dish, glass, and fistful of silver. As his left hand clutched the object, the cloth in his right swished, and swirled, and homed in on problem spots. Then the cloth would drop. Hot rinse water would gush from the tap for a few seconds while the left hand turned and twisted. That hand would then plunk the object onto the drainer. I tried to be fast and attentive in my drying, but I was able to get by without nearly as much attention. Dave had left me no dirty spots to deal with.

Careful attention raises the quality of what we do without necessarily slowing us down. If you take re-doing time into account, it probably takes less time.

I asked Dave to tell me what was behind his careful approach to doing things. He had several interesting things to say. First, he made it clear that maximizing quality is his first priority. When many of us face a sink full of dishes or a room that needs painting, getting the job done in minimum time is our first priority. Instead, Dave focuses on doing it right. To him the time it takes is secondary. The challenge is to do his best. "I don't put a time frame on things. That isn't important. Whether I've done a really good job *is*. The *final result* is what's important to me, not the time I spend. I want to do whatever I do in a quality way."

Part of doing a quality job, he feels, is thoroughly sizing up the situation before you start. When he and I did the dishes, it simply meant spending thirty seconds looking around the kitchen, assessing the task and the available resources, and then pondering possible courses of action until the clearly best way of handling things became apparent. In this situation all the necessary information was right there, but frequently it's not. For many people — especially men, I'm sorry to say — ego gets in the way at this point. Not being able to say, even to themselves, "I don't know," they fill in the blanks with guesses or unchecked assumptions and charge into action.

Dave does it differently: "I've discovered that you go to people who have the answers. People love to be asked to share what they know. Doing this minimizes screwups. It greatly improves the odds that I'll get it right." Dave calls it information gathering. He reviews the options, gathers information, and researches the situation in detail. He pre-plans, and doesn't necessarily take the first option or solution that presents itself.

The North American tendency is to divide the world and our individual lives into the important and the unimportant. Having made this neat division, we then pay much attention to the first and as little as we can get away with to the second. As I understand it, it's different in Japan. The Japanese don't slice the world up into important and unimportant. And the Japanese pay much attention to detail. To them, everything is important. They immerse themselves in the activity of the moment, whatever it may be, and treat the task at hand with care and attention.

I talked about careful doing with a friend who has lived in Japan for many years. "The Japanese have a word for it," she said, "*mame* [mah-may]. It means someone who does everything meticulously. In fact, the attitude 'Whatever you do, is worth doing well' pervades Japanese culture."

She went on to say that the level of the work doesn't matter; as many cleaners or brass polishers approach their work this way as artists, engineers, or business executives. She also shared with me a French saying that fits: "Il n'y a pas de sots métiers. Il n'y a que de sottes gens." *There are no stupid jobs; only stupid people.*

In conclusion, then, what can we say about the value of meticulous attention? First, there are fewer screwups. If we think about the major disasters in our lives, can't we attribute many of them to not paying enough attention to something? When we habitually pay attention, things go more smoothly.

Second, paying attention keeps us where the action is: the present moment. *Now* is the only time in which living can happen. When we pay attention to the activity of the moment we are alive. We feel good about what we're doing. When we don't pay attention, life passes us by.

Third, paying attention trains us to pay attention. The more we do it, the easier it is to do. Attentiveness breeds attentiveness.

And finally, when we pay attention to what we are doing, we are filled with a satisfaction that just isn't there when we deal with the bits and bubbles and dirty jobs of life with half a mind. When we pay close attention, quality goes up — the quality of what we do, what we make, and perhaps most important, the quality of our life experience.

5

Doing It Now

We all do it at times: we put off doing things until later. Whether or not this is harmful, and the degree of the harm, depends on the circumstances. It is a complex issue.

For some people, procrastination is a habitual coping behaviour triggered by a deeply felt need or fear, making it extremely tenacious and hard to get rid of. In its more extreme forms, procrastination can eventually lead to personal disaster of one kind or another, and for these people the solution lies in uncovering procrastination's roots — usually through psychological counselling or therapy.

For many other people procrastination raises its head only occasionally, and may be related to poor organizational habits, inattention, or relying too much on a memory that's not quite up to the demands being put on it. For these people the solution may simply be better time management and personal organization.

Procrastination is clearly a thicket; how can we make our way through it? In examining our own 'put-it-off-till-later' behaviour, we first need to ask if putting it off makes rational sense. Sometimes putting things off is totally appropriate. For one thing, it makes sense to put off doing something when there is a good chance that it might never need to be done at all. Examples of this occur frequently in the practice of law. Let's say that Mr. Jones sues Mr. Smith, and the case is scheduled to come to trial in two months. Neither party wants the expense of a trial, so during those two months their lawyers will try to negotiate an out-of-court settlement. In this situation it makes sense for both lawyers to put off detailed case preparation until the last minute. If they prepared their cases well before the court date, and then settled out of court, Jones and Smith would have to pay for legal work that ultimately would prove to be unnecessary.

Waiting also makes sense in situations where the best course of action has not yet become clear. In such situations we sometimes come across the opposite of procrastination. There are people who get very upset by uncertainty, and sometimes these people prematurely undertake a course of action just to ease their uncomfortable feelings. Bothered by not knowing, and by lack of action, they charge off too soon, and sometimes get themselves in as much trouble as habitual procrastinators do.

For those who do not have a deeply rooted psychological need to procrastinate, appropriate planning can often help. People who manage large, complex projects such as engineering development projects and building construction projects employ some techniques that can also be used by the rest of us to better organize our personal lives. Engineers and contractors create detailed charts which break the large project down into specific tasks, show the duration of each task, and arrange all the tasks in a suitable order. If, for example, the project is to build a house, the excavation must be done before the concrete foundation can be poured. The foundation must be in place before the wall framing can begin. The walls must be up before the roof joists can be put in place, etc. But later on, the plumbing and electrical wiring activities can go on at the same time. By

- listing a project's essential tasks,
- estimating the time required for each, and then
- arranging those tasks in a pattern of task-completion paths on a chart,

a task-oriented plan for getting the big job done is created.

Creating such a chart for our own projects undercuts procrastination in several ways. One reason people procrastinate is that the project they face seems overwhelming. There is this big amorphous thing that must be done, but where to start? Any starting point they might select, any individual task, seems so puny compared to the entire project. They find the whole thing daunting, and hold back.

To overwhelmingness we must often add fuzziness. In big-project situations we often do not have a clear picture of everything that is involved, or the order in which things must be done. Here, confusion leads to procrastination. By charting the project we cut through the confusion. We see each task and how the various tasks relate to each other in time. Clarity replaces fuzziness, and the overwhelming bigness is cut into accomplishment-sized pieces.

Forgetting is another cause of procrastination. Most of us lead very busy lives, and our memories are sometimes just not up to the demands we put on them. As a result, we fail to do things simply because we forget, and then forget again. The pocket notebook is a tool that can help us deal with the kind of not-doing that is rooted in memory lapses. For years I've carried around those little three-by-five-inch notebooks with the spiral binding along the top edge. First thing in the morning, I list the day's major tasks. Then, as the day progresses, I cross off items and add new ones. If something doesn't get done today, it goes on tomorrow's list.

These little notebooks are useful in other ways too. They provide a temporary storage place for good ideas, insights, and the miscellaneous data we come across during the day: names, addresses, telephone numbers, and the like. I call these notebooks *my paper brains*, and because I'm a writer who is always jotting down some priceless thought or other, when they get full I save them. Naturally, for this notebook idea to work, your neurological memory must work well enough to put things on the list in the first place, and then prompt you to look at the list from time to time during the day.

It's easy to make a case that procrastination is usually irrational. In most circumstances, putting things off simply makes no sense. The postponed work must eventually be done, and if one waits till the last minute there is a high probability that some sort of conflict will arise — and with it, stress.

Procrastination leaves no flexibility for handling the unexpected, and as a result, the quality of the work is likely to suffer.

At the same time, for those who have serious procrastination problems, merely pointing out the counter-productive side of procrastination accomplishes nothing. These people are already well aware of procrastination's damaging and illogical nature. It is coming to understand the real reason or reasons behind their procrastination that frees these procrastinators.

In their book, *Procrastination,*[5] therapists Jane Burka and Lenora Yuen present brief case studies of many procrastinators, and explore the roots of their procrastination. The authors conclude that people procrastinate for a variety of reasons:

- **Fear of failure, fear of not being as capable as they would like to be.** (If I procrastinate I know I haven't given the task my best effort. So if the results are not perfect, I can blame lack of time rather than any shortcomings in my own innate ability.)
- **Fear of success.** (Severe procrastination almost guarantees that you will not succeed.)
- **Fear of responsibility and independence.** (Procrastinating leads to missed deadlines and poor quality work, and this lessens the likelihood that you will be promoted or given more autonomy.)
- **Fear of attachment.** (Procrastination is a handy way of keeping others from getting too close. Arriving late for dates, not calling, and failing to keep promises works against annoying closeness. It helps maintain an interpersonal distance that feels safe.)

Procrastination, in its more pernicious forms, is a general-purpose, destructive behaviour that enables some people to cope with serious fears. Getting out of its grip often requires professional help. For those of us less seriously crippled by it, however, procrastination can be made to yield to logic, common sense, and a few tricks from the professionals who manage complexity for a living. Once we really begin to see the value of **doing it now** to both peace of mind and to the quality of our work, procrastination begins to lose its appeal. And through practice, it's possible to replace the put-it-off habit with the do-it-now habit.

6

Confident Knowing

Our decisions arise from a process involving the

1. values we hold dear, the
2. internalized information that we call *knowledge*, and
3. information about our immediate situation being supplied at this moment by our senses.

One problem with this process is that each specific item of knowledge seems to have a confidence level assigned to it when it is stored away in memory. It might be something like:

- Grade A information: Absolutely reliable; use confidently in making any sort of decision.
- Grade B information: Likely to be true; okay for general use, but not where your life depends on it.
- Grade C information: It sounds plausible; it might be true, but then again it might not be. Don't rely on it for anything important.

To make quality decisions we need quality knowledge — we need internalized information that inspires enough confidence to allow its use in all situations.

The situation would be clearer if the English language had four or five words, each of which reflected a different level of confidence in our knowing. Unfortunately, we have only that one word *know* to apply to all levels, and this tends to mask the underlying reality. Perhaps the A/B/C labels above will help. Labelled or not labelled, however, different confidence levels do exist. To live skilfully we must recognize this, and take steps to acquire information of the highest possible grade.

Several factors influence how confident we are that a statement is true:

- The clarity of the statement.
- The source of the statement.
- How well our previous intellectual learning supports the statement.
- How well our previous first-hand experience supports the statement.
- Whether the statement *feels* true.

Let's consider these five, one at a time.

Independent of whether or not a statement actually is true, the *clarity of the presentation* affects our confidence in its validity. For one thing, we're not likely to have much confidence in any statement we don't understand. At the other extreme, exceptionally clear and understandable statements tend to carry with them overtones of validity. We must be careful, however. Clarity is no *guarantee* of truth, and it is sometimes used to disguise half-truths or outright lies. We need to beware of simple assertions concerning complex issues, for example.

The *origin of the statement* also affects our degree of confidence. As the years go by each of us mentally compiles, and constantly revises, a list of information sources. We assign confidence ratings to those sources. We consider some of them to be reliable, some to be unreliable, and others to have major or minor biases. Some sources are widely respected by many people and appear on many lists — Einstein, for example, although few of us understand his work. For the most part, however, lists differ greatly from each other, and a reliable source on one list is likely to be considered an unreliable source on another. The Pope, for example, would appear on many lists, but confidence in the truth of Papal statements would vary from extremely high in some cases, to extremely low in others.

"*Is the statement supported by my own past intellectual learning?*" is another important consideration. Over time we acquire a lot of information, and from it we create a set of assumptions about the way things are — a set of beliefs about what is true and not true. If we come across a statement that clashes with this body of already-acquired information, we tend to greet it with skepticism because it conflicts with all this other information that we have come to trust.

How well a statement is supported by our own first-hand experience is perhaps most important of all. Much of our intellectually acquired knowledge is what I call *second-hand* knowledge. It is word-related knowledge picked up through schooling, reading, the electronic media, and what people have told us. It often ranks no more highly with us than an educated guess or a tentative hypothesis about things. I say this because when decision time comes we don't have enough confidence in much of this "knowledge" to base important life decisions on it. We give a much higher confidence level to knowledge the we acquire first hand or which is supported by our first-hand knowledge.

One more gauge of confidence is *our intuitive feeling about it.* Does the statement *feel* true or doesn't it? What is our intuitive, gut-level reaction to it? Intuitively felt truth is high-confidence truth, and we often believe this sort of knowing strongly enough to base major life decisions on it. Our intuitive process takes a lot into account in coming up with these simple *true* or *not true* feelings. Still, even a deeply felt sense of truth is not an infallible sign of it. If the intuitive process has received erroneous data, even this most holistic of mental processes can produce a misplaced feeling of confidence. Perhaps the highest level of trust exists when we encounter a statement that both rings true intellectually and feels true intuitively.

In real life, how does all this play out? What steps can we take to acquire truthful information, information in which we can have a high degree of confidence? One thing we can do is to upgrade the quality of our *second-hand information* — the information that arrives as words and pictures generated by others. One approach is to go on a personal search for new sources of information. Here we must actively expose ourselves — at least for a while — to much more information in our chosen areas of interest than we normally would. We must seek out and read new magazines and scholarly journals and books until a pattern begins to emerge for us. Certain sources will eventually rise above the rest; these, then, will be the prime candidates for our time and attention in the future.

When we can find no single source that is clearly superior, the best approach is probably to gather and compare information from multiple sources. The task here is to track down information sources — newsletters, magazines, journals, electronic journals on Internet, etc. — that have a variety of biases and slants, and to locate well-edited sources. There are now thousands of tightly focused newsletters and specialty magazines. There are even publications geared to helping you find them; two of my favourites are *Utne Reader*,[6] and *Whole Earth Review*.[7]

One thing to look for is editorial taste that you have confidence in, and this is likely to mean editorial taste that is similar to your own. Editors are paid to sort through masses of information and to publish the best of it. You don't have time to do this. But if you happen to find an editor with a mindset that inspires confidence, you have lucked out big time. It is wonderful to discover a publication that seems to be written just for you — to find in issue after issue that the editor's sense of what to include bears an uncanny congruity with your own.

Direct contact with knowledgeable people can be an important source of reliable information. As mentioned in the **Being a Learner** chapter (chapter 2), computer communication is an excellent way to get in touch with such people in almost any area of concern. The Internet's thousands of special-interest *Usenet News Groups* allow you to meet and communicate with others who share your interests.

Attending to the quality of the intellectual information that comes our way is important, but more important still is taking steps to acquire more of our knowledge directly. As I mentioned, we generally reserve our highest level of confidence for knowledge that is at least validated by our own direct experience. Especially where some future course of action depends on confidence in the knowledge we acquire, we need to make its acquisition in as direct and personally involved a way as possible. Among the techniques we can use are:

- **Do it yourself, attentively.** Here the idea is to develop understanding by doing the thing itself, by immersing ourselves in what we hope to understand. Where physical activity is involved, the necessity for this seems obvious. It's clear to everyone that you can't learn to dance the Highland Fling or become proficient at tennis simply by reading about these things. It's not quite as obvious with regard to spiritual practices and other personal growth activities, but here, too, reading just tells you what the real work is all about.

    Direct involvement also applies to selecting a career. Getting a taste of the work itself before spending many years in school could help prevent mismatches between people and livelihood. Could we in some sense pursue this potential career first as a hobby? (We could with electronics, flying, theatre, and music, for example.) Or would volunteering to do a stint of related work without pay be possible?

- **Go there yourself, attentively.** Sometimes the essential knowing requires our presence. We may need to talk with someone personally. Or we may need to immerse ourselves in the atmosphere of a *place* and let our intuitive process absorb all of that subtle stuff which is beyond words. If I am considering a move to another city I might read a host of books and articles about it, but I probably would not want to move there permanently without visiting it first.

- **Use your intuitive process more effectively.** Intuition's resources are immense and its processing is sophisticated, but its outputs are simple, subtle, and easy to miss. This non-verbal, reality-seeking, problem-solving process is always on hand to help us. It seems to take everything into account in its efforts to be helpful. And if we cooperate with it, our intuitive process can lead us to startling insights about our lives and the cosmos, and to creative outpourings well beyond those of our ego-driven intellect.

The starting point here is to consciously recognize your intuitive process and to honour it. The cooperation consists primarily of

- a respectful attitude toward it,
- a conscious "listening" for its messages, and
- a quieting of our minds so that its subtle, quiet responses are not drowned out by the busy buzzy activities of the thinking, planning, remembering verbal mind.[8]

In summary, crafting a satisfying life requires more than simply acquiring a lot of information and making it our own. It also requires that the information we acquire be high-grade information, information that inspires confident use in all situations.

7

Our Engagement with Work

These days, most of us adults have a job that we work at for pay. We do something someone else wants done, and receive money in return. Even if we are self-employed, we are doing something for other people. There will be clients to satisfy, or customers. For some people their work is their life, deserving nothing less than total commitment. For others, work is an onerous necessity — deserving only minimal effort. Where does wisdom reside in all this? Is there an optimally skilful way to view our relationship with paid work? Let me share with you *Cop's Game Theory of Employment.*

There are many things we can choose to do with our lives, there are many games we can choose to play. Some of these games have an economic pay-off for the players; others don't. Some, like art, music, and sports have an economic pay-off for only a few highly skilled players. Not many of us are skilled enough to be paid for doing art, music, or sports. We might paint pictures for fun, play music for fun, or play hockey for fun, but for almost all of us, those games won't buy our groceries or pay the mortgage.

The way things are in our society, we are expected to prepare ourselves to play some economic game that has enough pay-off to support ourselves. And we are expected to play that game with at least the minimum required level of skill, energy, and commitment. People who can't or won't do this are not quite condemned by our culture to freeze and starve, but life is not bountiful or easy for them. Things are made especially difficult for those who are capable of working, but won't.

At this point in our social evolution very few people are able to make a decent living doing exactly what they want to do. It's too bad, but that's the way it is. As a result, we compromise. In our jobs we look for some combination of interest, excitement, challenge, working conditions, work duration, security, and economic pay-off that we can live with. At the same time, we don't always love the economic game we finally agree to play.

When we take a job, however, we are really signing on with a team, and agreeing to play a certain game. The game has rules and standards of play, even though those things are not always explicitly stated. If we were getting paid to play a game like hockey, each game and each personal statistic would be a reminder about minimum standards — even if the coach and manager said nothing, which is unlikely. In most jobs, however, the boss does not remind us daily about minimum standards. Yet standards exist, and after working at any job for a while we get to know what they are. Furthermore, unless we meet those minimum standards the boss will someday fire us, and the paycheck from that source will stop.

Many employers would recoil at the idea of employees looking at their jobs as games — in part because it conflicts with the employer's secret hope of getting total dedication and unlimited commitment from the employee. They would lose little by taking the game view, however, and perhaps even gain. In part because employers no longer honour their side of the traditional *work hard and you'll always have a job here* bargain, fewer people these days live just to work. Facing that is simply being realistic. Yet it is also realistic to expect employees to play the game for which they were hired, in accord with a reasonable set of rules, terms, and conditions. It is reasonable to expect them to apply their energy and attention to the job while they're on the job. From early childhood on we've been involved with games, and we all know what fair play is. The game metaphor helps us look at the working world from a fair-play perspective.

The game metaphor also helps us look at jobs with an appropriate level of seriousness. Because *The Job* plays a central, multi-faceted role in our culture, some people are intensely serious about their jobs. The job is for them the centre of their lives; it takes first priority most of the time. Naturally, employers love this kind of attitude and do their best to cultivate and reinforce it. At the other extreme there are people whose jobs have very little importance to them. Many of these people move from job to job, and a few eventually luck into some job situation that couples a regular paycheck with few demands. Both extremes strike me as unfortunate for the employee. In the first situation, the individual's life is intense but narrow. In the second, the individual is just putting in time, trading half their waking life for economic survival, with no other benefits coming from that expenditure of time. Treating the job as a game helps us avoid both pitfalls.

One reason that the game metaphor fits the working situation is that games are both serious and not serious. Games are intense and serious enterprises while they are being played, yet once over, games are easily and quickly put aside and forgotten. In the job-as-game view of work, jobs are intense and serious enterprises during working hours, but once this day's inning is over, it is appropriate to put the job aside.

Job-as-game fits well with the Eastern idea of living intensely in the present moment. When it's time to work, we work. When it's time to socialize, we socialize. When it's time to wash dishes, we wash dishes. In the Eastern view, this moment's activity is worthy of being addressed with full energy and attention, whatever that activity happens to be. Each activity is worthy of the same wholehearted spirit that we normally bring to the playing of a game.

We all know what happens if we don't bring a wholehearted spirit to a game: The game is spoiled; there is no point playing. Did you ever play cards or volleyball or some other game with a person who didn't really want to play, or who didn't respect the rules? The non-enthusiast spoils the game for everyone. Games, by their very nature, demand energetic, attentive engagement. In the same way, people who don't energetically play the workplace game they have committed themselves to play often spoil the game for their coworkers.

In any field, the game we are paid to play may eventually get boring. Or we may play intensely for a while and then burn out. Fair enough; these things happen. If our present problem is boredom or burnout, we might look for an answer in one of several directions. Our first approach might be to take a fresh look at the present work situation. Is there some way of modifying the game itself, or the way we play it, to make it more rewarding — more interesting, exciting, challenging, or fun? The powers-that-be in many organizations are open to such suggestions.

A second approach is simply to switch games. As I mentioned, one of the realities of our present age and culture is that most adults must play at least one economic game, and play it at an acceptable level. There are many of these games, each with its set of pluses and minuses. If the current game has ceased to be your game, and you don't have a trust fund or other independent means of support, there's probably no long-term alternative but to find another game.

Perhaps we find ourselves in a job for which we have no enthusiasm at all, yet one we feel we can't leave. No, that's not quite right. There is no job we couldn't leave if we were willing to face the consequences. Let's say, instead, that leaving this job would disrupt so much else in our lives that staying with it, at least for now, makes some kind of sense. How do we deal with a situation like this?

One approach is to redefine the game we are playing. Besides the paycheck, what is going on in the workplace that might be of value to us? Are there skills that we could learn if we put ourselves out a little more? Is there possibly some experienced and relatively wise person in the organization who might be open to mentoring us?

Let's say that this kind of exploration comes to nothing. The co-workers are all nasty or lazy, the working environment is abominable, and the job itself is either totally boring, or demands every bit of energy we've got. Hopeless? Not if we uplevel the game. We can always redefine our game to be *the personal growth game.* From the personal growth perspective that horrible job situation was crafted by fate and presented to us as a magnificent gift. It is an ideal environment for putting our budding attempts at conscious growth to the test. If we define the primary game of our life to be that of growing in love and wisdom, then every life activity becomes a sub-game. Each becomes a laboratory of active play in which we put our present knowledge and wisdom to the test, and in which we further develop our ability to love and act wisely. Teacher after teacher has pointed out that any situation we have trouble accepting is an indicator of still-needed growth — as well as a workshop where that growth can take place.

Throughout our adult lives this matter of work and livelihood will be an ongoing issue. And if our aim is to constantly refine our life, we will be constantly refining our livelihood. There will be times to leave and times to stay, but never a time when attentive engagement with the work itself is inappropriate.

8

Appropriate Planning

I, by natural tendency, am a list-maker, a decider-in-advance, a planner. Early in my adult life I found that I accomplished more in a day if I made a list of the things I needed to do. And in my working life as a design engineer, it became quite clear that if I didn't plan the next nine-month development project in considerable detail, the nine months would be over and I would have nothing to show — except, perhaps, one trashed career.

There is, however, a danger connected with planning. We who see its great power for good in so many situations sometimes assume that planning makes sense in *all* situations. We natural planners sometimes let planning expand into areas of life where it just doesn't belong.

Part of effective living involves assessing situations, and then matching the kind and amount of planning to the needs of the situation. To make all this clearer, let's look at what appropriate planning might mean in three contexts: *projects, travel,* and *our lives.*

Projects can be underplanned, overplanned, or appropriately planned. Underplanned projects turn out to be full of surprises because the whole happening has not been thought through in advance. They take longer and cost more than appropriately planned ones. In addition, the chaos level goes up, there are frequent crises, and everyone involved is subjected to more stress.

Underplanning destroys any hope of an orderly work environment.

Overplanning a project reduces the ability to deal with the unexpected. It would be foolish, for example, to plan the construction of a house to the point where the start and completion dates for all facets of the job are cast in stone. If we try that, we're headed for trouble. Perhaps the concrete-form people tell us that it will take two days to get the plywood forms ready for the concrete foundation. Sounds good, so we go ahead and schedule the concrete truck to arrive at 8:00 a.m. on the morning of day three. But what if it actually takes three days to put the forms in place? If that concrete truck arrives right on schedule, somebody has a big problem. Wet concrete is not patient. Overplanning destroys flexibility.

Appropriately planning a project means thinking out in advance those aspects of the project that are amenable to that, and making advance provision for decisions that we must defer. An appropriately planned project will embody a sane working environment, few panic situations, few unexpected costs, and few delays for which we can't compensate. The time and energy that might otherwise go into laying excessively rigid plans goes instead into project monitoring, creating backup plans whenever there is a hint of a potential problem, and maintaining flexibility.

Recreational travel is sometimes underplanned, but more often it is overplanned. Many people would not think of heading off on a trip without advance hotel or motel reservations for every night's stay. Doing this makes perfect sense if you are heading off at the peak of high season into a prime tourist area which is known to have too few accommodations. But does it really make sense most of the time? Often, booking rooms in advance simply costs us more and ties us down, eliminating opportunities for serendipity and adventure, and leaving us with less money to spend on fun. The less expensive hotels, motels, and pensions don't advertise or have 800 numbers. But when you arrive in a place, this other, cheaper option usually exists. Guidebooks geared to the budget traveler are now available for most locales, and most libraries have copies of the more general accommodation guides that travel agents use. These books can help us discover in advance those times and places where advance reservations would make sense, and they point the way to the cheap places once we get there.

Another vacation overplanning problem arises if someone in the family feels the need to plan each day's activities in advance. For many people, a tightly planned vacation isn't a vacation. Having to adhere to a timetable is just not relaxing, and it kills spontaneity and adventure.

Where travel and leisure are concerned, appropriate planning is very often minimum planning. Yes, you need a rough idea of where you want to go and what you want to do. And certain key items of transportation, accommodation, and recreation may need to be booked in advanced. But in my experience, lightly planned travel is lots more fun than heavily planned travel.

What about the planning of our lives? What level of planning is appropriate here? It helps if we separate, in our thinking, the structural aspects of our lives from the moment-to-moment stuff. By structural I mean the important long-term, slow-to-change elements of our lives such as livelihood, important relationships, activities in pursuit of learning, commitments to serve others, and the practices that affect our physical, psychological, and spiritual well-being. Relying on chance rather than choice to set up this life framework may be all too common, but it is not apt to result in the most satisfying possible life. To pursue our life goals, actualize our potentials, and express our deepest values, we need to set up a matrix of structural elements which is compatible with them and helps us realize them. This requires planning, and energetically following through with those plans.

Within this structure of our lives, daily life happens. It is within the lattice of structural elements that we hang out. It is here that we live, and here that we need to be more selective about planning. Here, too, it is possible to underplan. When there is no planning, some things inevitably remain undone, and things undone often have negative consequences. Underplanning also wastes time, and certain kinds of underplanning tend to raise the chaos level and the frequency of crises. We must eventually do our chores, yet when we don't work them into the day with forethought we often find that the most convenient circumstances for doing them have passed. If we make a list and everything is on it, one shopping trip does it all. If we fail to consider the total situation beforehand, we must make extra trips.

It is also possible to overplan our daily lives. It may make sense to make a list of things that need doing, but much of the time it is appropriate to just let the moment-to-moment actuality unfold. The challenge for us control and planning freaks in living moment to moment is to get out of that I-must-control-everything mindset, and learn to go with the flow. Letting go of the need to control isn't easy; but with practice, we can learn to do it. And in doing it we begin to experience a more relaxed state of mind.

If the planning and controlling rational mind is able to back off sufficiently, a new possibility opens up: letting the wise intuitive process direct our day. Our intuitive side is that quiet, non-verbal, value-centred, big-picture process that communicates with the verbal side of us in various ways: Sometimes through yes/no feelings, sometimes through those feelings of direction we call *hunches*, sometimes through insightful changes in perspective, and occasionally in *Aha!* experiences where we suddenly see the solution to some problem.

We might begin the day with a period of quiet reflection, during which we go over what must be done that day. (Those of us with poor memories will want to write some of this down.) All of us, good memories or bad, can then let go of the need for me/I/ego/self to get it all done. We can, instead, let the wisdom within, the intuitive process, dictate the specifics of our actions as the day unfolds. In this mode we simply keep doing what the unfolding situation calls for. We might occasionally ask the wisdom: "What's highest priority now?" and then wait for some feeling of direction. If priorities switch in the middle of a job, we switch jobs. Above all, we do not bulldoze through the day, following a rigid plan, nor do we let the day drift mindlessly away. We remain alert, attentive, ready to act, and ready for the next subtle message from the intuitive process. Even in the midst of action, the aim is to maintain a quiet attentiveness.

In short, most of us could benefit by looking with fresh eyes at how we handle planning. We can change our present underplanning or overplanning habits. We can learn to do the kind and amount of planning that's appropriate for each situation.

9

Seeking the Truth

There is a reality. The universe functions in certain ways and not others, for instance. And you and I behave in various ways in various circumstances. Truth, as I am using the term, is human understanding that is in accord with reality, with what actually is. Understanding that is absent (ignorance) and understanding that is not in accord with reality (delusion) create all sorts of problems in our lives. Analysis that is not based on truth misleads us, and action that is not based on truth goes awry. A high-quality life, a life that functions smoothly, is a life based on understanding the way things are and the way things work.

Do we want to know the truth about ourselves? About the world around us? About our place in the cosmos?

"Of course," is the automatic response.

"Yes and no," is the reality.

We humans are comfort-loving creatures. We are also curious creatures. If our curiosity was never in conflict with our love of comfort, curiosity would take the reins, and many more of us would absorb ourselves in truth-seeking, reality-seeking explorations. Unfortunately, there is often conflict. Some truths upset us. They disturb our comfort.

For the most part, this conflict arises in two kinds of situations. In the first, some newly acquired understanding conflicts with our existing world view, with our normal way of interpreting and making sense of the data of life. In the second, we see something about ourselves that runs counter to the image we have of ourselves — counter to our assumptions about the kind of person we are — our values, our behaviour.

Let's first consider the world view problem. Each culture has its *consensus reality*, its set of assumptions about the way things are that represents truth in the overall judgement of that culture. As each of us grows up we acquire our own world view. These individual world views mirror consensus reality in many respects, but not all. To some extent we develop our own set of assumptions about how things are and how things work, as well as about what is valuable and what is not. Parents, friends, school, church, and personal experience all influence the process, and slowly, gradually, we create for ourselves an interpretive framework that helps us make sense of the raw data of life. My world view is in many respects similar to yours, but even in a shared culture, many of the specifics will differ.

We need a world view. It helps us get through a day and a lifetime. Yet that world view can also limit us. In combining many helpful, truth-fostering ways of looking at things with some misleading perspectives and at least a few outright lies, it is a mixed blessing. There are no perfectly accurate world views.

We get considerable comfort from the feeling that we understand. When, however, something conflicts with our world view — when we are presented with new information about the way things are, or we are asked to interpret old data in a new way — discomfort often arises. This clash between our experience and our assumptions about truth is a form of cognitive dissonance. The level of that discomfort, and our way of dealing with it, depends largely upon how attached we have become to our present world view — how tightly we cling to it.

Some people clutch their world view very tightly and resist accepting any data that would force them to change it, no matter how persuasive the case for change might be. These people have become ego-attached to their habitual way of looking at things, and they interpret a threat to their point of view as a threat to themselves. Rigid, reactive, and closed-minded is the way they appear to others.

At the other end of the spectrum we find wise, open-minded, reality-seeking people. Such people have come to the conclusion that their *long-term* comfort is going to be greatest if they understand what *is* as clearly as possible. This requires being open to new data and new ways of interpreting data. It requires updating their world view whenever they come upon a better, clearer, truer way of looking at things. They also understand that there are limits to our knowledge. When they don't know, they acknowledge that they don't know. They don't fill in the blanks with guesses and call it truth.

Wise, reality-seeking people also have moments of cognitive dissonance, but their way of dealing with it is very different. Instead of rejecting the new data or perspective in knee-jerk fashion, and immediately mounting a heated defence of their way of seeing things, reality-seeking people risk immersing themselves in the new. Instead of immediately pushing the new idea away, they intentionally move toward it, get into it, try to understand it. Only after they have clearly understood it, do they set it up against the old established "truth" and ultimately accept or reject it. Their desire for clarity and truth is stronger than their desire to avoid discomfort. Also, even when the discomfort exists, it is a less intense discomfort because open-minded people are less ego-attached to their world views. They are less personally identified with them. Sure, like everyone else, their world views form part of their personhood, but they are not afraid of becoming a different person if different means better. And they believe that ways of understanding which are truer, which reflect reality more accurately, are definitely better.

There is another set of assumptions that we carry around with ourselves — a very personal one. It is often called our self-image. Whereas our world view helps us make sense of the external world, our self-image is a picture of the person we believe ourselves to be. The self-image, like the world view, is also the product of years of living and a multitude of influences — parents, siblings, school, friends, etc. Also like the world view, it is not a completely true picture of the way things are. Some people, for instance, have acquired an overly negative self-image. They've become convinced that they have few endearing qualities. They may see themselves as physically unattractive, uncreative, unproductive, or dumb. And with such a self-image in place, they tend to ignore and downplay messages from the world which say that they are better than all that. Because they don't see things as they are, their unrealistic view of themselves gets in the way of their effectiveness and their growth.

Others of us have an overly positive image of ourselves. The image we cherish and carry around is of the person we want to become rather than the person we are. Like the too-negative self-image, the too-positive one also interferes with our growth. If we have come to feel that we are perfect, then we avoid acknowledging any behaviour, thoughts, or values that fall short of the ideal. If we become attached to a perfect self-image, then discrepancies between reality and perfection cause inner distress, and the brain/mind process sometimes goes to extreme lengths to avoid that pain. It may *rationalize* the less-than-perfect reality — explain it away by creating a plausible but incorrect reason for it happening. It may *deny* its existence. It may *repress* the memory of it having happened. Or it may *project* it onto others – that is, cause us to see our own negative behaviours as flaws in other people. These *defense mechanisms*, as they are called, are ways in which the mind lies to itself to avoid discomfort. But these lies cause a much deeper kind of hurt. What we are unable to see, we can't possibly change. So the goal must be to see ourselves **as we really are**, right now, today – the good, the bad, the ugly – all of it. Seeing things as they are is the starting point for any sort of personal transformation.

Is there anything we can do to move from delusion about what *is*, to seeing things as they really are? Of course there is. The first step is to sincerely want to do something about it. We must want to understand what is really going on, even if the reality we find disappoints us in some way. This can be tough. Can we value reality more highly than our hopes? More highly than our expectations? Can we value reality even if it overturns certain long-held, emotionally cherished assumptions? Intellectually deciding that clarity and truth are better than delusion probably will not automatically change closed-mindedness to open, or overturn a deeply entrenched need to be perfect. It is, however, an appropriate place to start.

We can also adopt a new attitude toward psychic discomfort. When new data conflicts with self-image or world view, and discomfort arises, we can change the way we respond to that discomfort. Instead of trying to push the discomfort away and get rid of it as quickly as possible, we can consider it to be a helpful message saying, "Look more closely at this. Exactly why is it that you are feeling uncomfortable?" When we feel the cognitive dissonance it means that we have seen something, so let's look squarely at it. Let's actively investigate the disturbance.

There is something else we can do. We can become more attentive, detached, and quiet-minded. The moments when reality and self-image clash are often fleeting ones. Often, an intention to act flashes through the mind, and action immediately follows. Perhaps an impulse of anger arises, and angry words escape our lips. We may not be attentive enough to see what has actually happened, to see the step-by-step process that led up to, and resulted in, our overt behaviour, our harsh speech. Yet we can train ourselves to be more attentive. We can cultivate the kind of quiet, attentive mind that makes such seeing more likely. Yoga, Tai Chi, and Mindfulness meditation are all practices that ground us in the present moment and call on us to be attentive to what is happening here and now. Through such practices we become increasingly able to catch the content of each fleeting moment, to see what our mind/body process is really up to.

When we become more accepting of truth-caused discomfort and our own imperfections, things start to get better.

- For one thing, we're not fighting reality any longer; we're cooperating with it. In any battle between reality and delusion, reality ultimately wins. And the fighting itself is uncomfortable.
- For another, seeing our own unskilful behaviour often starts a subtle process to get rid of it. If we haven't seen it, it isn't apt to change. But when we have seen it, the deeper wisdom within starts moving us toward new habits of mind and behaviour in which old, unskilful ways no longer have a place.

10

Feeling Good about Ourselves

Let's go more deeply into this matter of a negative self-image. The truth is that while some people feel good about themselves, many others do not. Why is this? And are there effective steps that we can take to correct a negative sense of self-esteem and self-worth?

Abraham Maslow considered esteem to be a primary human need. As he saw it, before we can become all we are capable of becoming we must be respected by others and respect ourselves. There is, of course, no way to control how others feel about us. Whether or not they give us compliments and strokes is strictly up to them. On the other hand, isn't it *self-esteem* that really matters here? Isn't the important thing *how we feel about ourselves?* And at least potentially, how we feel about ourselves *is* within our control. If self-esteem is the real problem, then we don't have to wait helplessly for someone else to save us.

Much of the research on self-esteem has involved children. That makes sense because it is when people are young that their first assumptions about self-worth are formed. Our early feelings about ourselves were shaped largely by parents, teachers, and playmates. Later, influences from advertising, electronic entertainment, and employers further affected our sense of self-esteem and helped shape the way we currently feel about ourselves.

Today, if we are parents, grandparents, teachers — or otherwise have contact with children — we can do much to help them value themselves simply by giving them our attention and our respect. As one author has eloquently pointed out,[9] we all want and need attention, and if children (and others) don't receive it as a freely given gift, they have their ways of getting it. When we pay attention to someone it confirms their significance and helps foster within them a positive response to life. **Attention and encouragement may be the most valuable things we can give to other people.**

We are no longer children. We either grew up in a supportive milieu or we didn't; that's history. What was, was, and our only option now is to move on from where we are at this moment. Research on developing self-esteem in adulthood is less abundant than the self-esteem research on children, but it does seems clear that it is possible for adults to change the estimate of self worth that they have formed. Psychological counselling or psychotherapy is the approach that is often suggested, and studies indicate that it can help improve self-esteem. This may be the best approach if feelings of low-self-worth are severe and pervade most areas of one's life. Self-help books are another possibility.[10] Where the problem is less severe (involving just one or a few areas of one's life) the following reflections might prove helpful.

Often, bad feelings about ourselves have a specific focus. We may feel rather good about ourselves generally, but perceive one or two upsetting flaws. Perhaps we don't consider ourselves smart, or don't feel particularly knowledgeable or creative. Perhaps the perceived flaw is physical: we don't feel attractive, or we don't feel athletically capable. Then again, we might feel morally or ethically flawed — disturbed by the way we are currently treating others or have treated them in the past. Assuming we feel deeply bothered in one of these areas, what steps can we take?

Appropriate action can come out of seeing the situation as it really is — seeing it through the clear lens of rational assessment rather than through the dark glass of emotional evaluation. The person with a poor self-image, by definition, sees problems, sees flaws. These flaws are real to the individual who feels deficient, but do others also see them? And if others do, are they seen to be a problem? Often they are not.

Some people see moral flaws where — rationally — there are none.

Perhaps the "flaw" is simply residual guilt from some off-the-wall moral trip laid on the child by parents or church. On the other hand, perhaps we actually have harmed others. In that case, acknowledging this to ourselves is appropriate — but that is very different from seeing ourselves as being morally flawed forever in some fundamental way. In any event, trying to come to grips with the situation *as it really is* is the first order of business.

Let's begin with the perceived problem of not being smart enough or knowledgeable or creative enough. These are really three separate issues:

- Smarts, intelligence, and giftedness all refer to our ability to learn.
- How knowledgeable we are refers to how much we have already learned, how much we currently know.
- Creativity refers to our ability to synthesize, to produce what never before existed, to solve problems in new ways.

As pointed out in chapter 1, the latest theory about intelligence debunks the traditional idea that there is one overall intelligence that determines the level of our potential in all areas of life. We saw that there are several different kinds of intelligence, and each of us is endowed with these different kinds to different degrees. After almost six decades of living I have concluded that I am mildly challenged musically and athletically. I have noted that whenever I undertook some course of musical development, or attempted to develop an athletic skill, I progressed more slowly than most others in my situation, and in the end was less proficient. Am I crushed by this? Has this ruined my life? No, not at all. Music and athletics are simply not my strong points. My talents — my gifts if you will — lie in other areas, and it is toward developing them that I have decided to devote most of my time and energy. Once it sinks in that we are not just dumb or smart, but smart at some things and less smart at others, we can look at ourselves afresh. We can dump the *dumb* label that we picked up somewhere, and pay attention to developing our strengths.

If lack of knowledge is the cause of our low self-esteem, the solution is straightforward: move the acquisition of knowledge to a higher place on our personal priority list. I faced this situation when, at age thirty, I realized that I had willingly imprisoned myself in the narrowness of an engineering career for the previous dozen years, and awoke to a wonderful, exciting world that I had been missing. I had just met several intellectually alive, interesting people who felt at home in this larger world and knew a great deal about it. I felt awed by them, and quite intimidated. They knew so much; I knew so little. What did I do? For the next year I spent most evenings and part of each weekend reading. As a result, my interests broadened. I became more knowledgeable about more things, and that intense feeling of intellectual inferiority gradually faded away. I had to commit a lot of time to the task, but the process itself was straightforward and risk-free: Put in the time, and you become more knowledgeable. That's all there is to it.

Feeling bad because we feel uncreative is a more complex matter. There are things that we can do, however, to enhance creativity, and I go into the matter in some detail in chapter 19, **Enhancing Creativity**.

What if a lack of physical attractiveness is causing self-image and self-worth problems? There are three approaches:

1.   **Fix it.** These days there is almost always something we can do to improve our appearance. We can have our hair cut or shaped or coloured. We can have our teeth whitened or capped or straightened. We can lose fat and develop muscle by changing the way we exercise and eat. A warning, though, about physical appearance. Plastic surgeons report that for some of their patients, changing the physical image does not change the mental image that they have of themselves. So we need to ask ourselves, "Is my appearance the real problem?" and be open to an answer that we have not wanted to hear.

2.   **Accept it.** For some the answer is to say, "Well this is just the way it is, and that's okay." They are then free to put all that bound-up personal appearance energy into activities that have a greater pay-off. They might work on becoming a warm and loving person, for example. Those who are successful at that task discover that they are loved in return by a multitude of people,

and that the physical appearance issue fades into insignificance.

3.   **Switch your attention from what you don't have to what you do have.** In appearance, as in other areas of life, each of us has strengths and weaknesses. A general tendency of people with a bad self-image is to pay attention to their weaknesses and ignore their strengths. The game here is to do just the opposite. Yes, the donut has a hole, but it is still mostly donut. Yes, the glass is half empty; but it is also half full. Taking a positive slant on things makes you feel better, and is empowering.

Finally, how about feelings of moral deficiency — feelings that I am, in some sense, a bad person?

- First we must honestly assess if we are harming others. If we are, then that must stop. And we may need help to do that.
- Second we must honestly assess if we are harming ourselves. If we are, then that, too, must stop. And here, also, we may need help.
- If we are not harming others or ourselves, then what's the problem? If there was real harm in the past we can think about the possibility of making amends. If, however, there is nothing we can realistically do now to compensate for what we did in the past, then learning from it and letting it go is probably the most skilful thing we can do. Continuing to wallow in remorse about it gets us nowhere.
- Coming to understand more clearly how the human decision-making process works can also be helpful. Our decisions don't arise magically from nowhere; they are our brain's response to a complex present situation and a complex matrix of past influences. Each decision that we make is the brain's best call about what course of action is optimum. As a result, **all of us, all the time, are doing the best we can.**

Sartre and the other French Existentialists hit on something very important with their stress on living a *meaningful* life. Does your life *matter?* Does mine? Do they matter to other people? Do they matter in the larger scheme of things? *Significance* may be the ultimate issue, as well as an important yardstick of successful living. Our feelings of self-worth are intimately tied to our sense of significance. What gives the strongest boost to our feelings of self-worth? Isn't it the knowledge that we are making a meaningful contribution to the world around us? That we are helping others? That we are doing things which somehow matter? When we are engaged in activities that we consider meaningful, strong positive feelings arise. We feel good about ourselves *because we know that our lives matter.*

11

Dealing with Reactivity

Hate, anger, lust, jealousy, wanting, and fear are powerful emotions that all too often lead to reactive behaviour and suffering for ourselves and others. Must we allow reactive emotions to run our lives? Of course not. But transcending their tendency to control our actions is not trivially easy. We must cultivate skilful ways of dealing with them, and this is made easier if we understand the role that these heavy-duty emotions play, and why they evolved.

We are told that most animal species — including insects, amphibians, birds, and reptiles — have no emotions. In the animals that evolved early on, like amphibians, a small range of simple perceptions give rise quite automatically to a few well-defined behaviours. Picture a frog sitting on a lily pad. Although the visual landscape registers optically on the retinas of the frog's eyes, frog neurology responds only to *changes* in the scene. If a small dark object moves across the frog's field of vision (a fly, perhaps?) the frog's tongue automatically darts out in that direction, and perhaps a fly is caught. And if there is a sudden overall darkening (the approach of a hawk, perhaps?) the frog automatically jumps off the lily pad into the water. There is no complex thinking process involved here, it seems, just a visual system designed for food detection on the one hand, and danger detection on the other — but not very discriminating about either. All small moving things are interpreted as food, and every sudden decrease in overall light level is interpreted as threat. Given either stimulus, the frog's response is automatic and predictable.

As animal life got more complex, however, more discriminating kinds of perception and a much wider range of behaviours evolved. This, in turn, created pressure to evolve brains that could process the much-increased flow of data. When the number of significant stimuli and responses rises to a high number, the number of possible *combinations* becomes astronomical. To complicate the matter further, priorities must be sorted out and conflicts must be resolved *very quickly*. (If there is a lion on the path behind you and a snake in front of you, you can't afford much time for situation evaluation and decision making.) As the number of combinations increased, it became increasingly difficult for brains to process the data quickly enough.

A way around the data-computation bottleneck evolved. It is widely believed that subjective experience in general, and selective attention in particular, began to play an active role in the decision-making process. Brains evolved that gave rise to complex *minds*, to subjective displays of data involving sight, sound, touch, taste, and odour — all simultaneously displayed in one mental "place." Selective attention is a feature of these complex minds. When attention focuses on a specific item of mind content, the brain generates neuronal data concerning that item. This data is available to mechanical, unconscious brain processes. We do not yet understand the details, but it does seem clear that this new mental/physical approach allowed complexity to increase while still maintaining acceptable speed, and kept to a manageable level the amount of computation the brain needed to do.

Strong emotions were another part of evolution's solution to this decision-making and behaviour-guiding problem. In a frog, the automatic reaction to a perceived opportunity or danger is the action itself: go after the fly, jump off the lily pad. In a human being the automatic reaction to an opportunity or danger is likely to be an *emotion* rather than a direct action. Emotions are messages that *suggest* or *promote* certain kinds of action, but they don't initiate action directly. Instead, emotions appear on the screen of the mind along with perceptions, thoughts, and other forms of mental data. The message that an emotion presents is taken into account by the situation-evaluation and decision-making process, but it is just one of many pieces of data being considered.

Let's imagine a situation that illustrates this. It's a hot day and you are walking down the sidewalk past an ice cream vendor. There, not three feet away, you see a delicious-looking ice cream bar. If our behaviour was hard-wired like the frog's behaviour, the sight of the ice cream might automatically lead to grabbing it and eating it, no matter what else was happening. In humans, however, seeing ice cream does not automatically trigger ice-cream-eating behaviour. Instead, seeing ice cream often triggers that mental experience we might call *ice cream lust*. A feeling of wanting arises in the mind, a desire to taste ice cream and feel its coolness.

This experience, however, may be just one of several experiences that simultaneously share space on the wide screen of awareness. As such, it will be just another piece of data that the brain takes into account when deciding what our behaviour should be.

Under ordinary circumstances ice cream lust might lead to a few spoken words, then to an exchange of money, and finally to ice cream entering your mouth. But let's imagine that just as the transaction starts to take place, a two-year-old boy runs past you into the street. On the awareness-screen of your mind the desire for the ice cream is still displayed, but now that screen also contains the image of a child in grave danger. Your attention goes to the image of the child, and within a fraction of a second

- this new information is taken into account by your brain,
- a new priority is established (snatch the child from the path of oncoming cars), and
- you find yourself in motion, stepping toward the little boy and reaching out to grab him.

A desire is a message that *advocates* action of a particular kind, but it is not an *imperative* to act. The desire for ice cream was present, and strong, but the brain decided to ignore that desire. **Wanting (or anger, hate, or fear for that matter) is simply a message, a suggestion that can be followed or ignored** — and in our example above, was ignored.

Dire emergencies are not the only situations where saying no to a reactive emotion makes sense. Take our desire for sweets, for example. Sugars are converted fairly directly into energy, and are nutritionally quite valuable. They had survival value for people, and through evolution's sifting and sorting of biological characteristics, human beings acquired a liking for foods that tasted sweet. Whenever sweet things were encountered, a message of desire appeared on people's mental screens: "Sweet. Good. Eat." In many hunter-gatherer situations sweet things were not abundant, so it made nutritional sense to act on that message at every opportunity. In the pre-technological world, an urge to eat sweets was a fairly reliable message about what to do, a fairly reliable prescription for action.

Today, things are different. Sweets are no longer rarities. Countless factories now churn out more candy and cookies and ice cream than is healthy for us to consume. Yet our built-in system of desires hasn't changed. We remain genetically programed to desire sweets, and many of us, much of the time, respond to that desire by eating them.

From one perspective, fear, hate, anger, jealousy, sexual lust, the desire for sweets — and all other forms of wanting what we don't have and wanting to get rid of what we do have — are powerful experiences. Functionally, however, **they are just informational messages about the present situation** — messages that happen to arrive in feeling-tinged form. They are warnings about some perceived or anticipated danger, or they are prods to take advantage of some perceived opportunity. They are messages that once helped individual humans survive and reproduce, and helped the human race avoid extinction. Today, however, they are alerting signals that are no longer trustworthy because the circumstances of life have changed so drastically. They still deserve to be considered when evaluating situations and making action decisions, but they should not be considered either absolute truths or imperatives to act. Even the most powerful desires and aversions are **just feeling-coated information** that we can take into account, and then either act upon or ignore.

Learning to say no to inappropriate urges increases our inner freedom immensely. *We need to evaluate sensations, feelings, and emotions for their underlying informational content, not for their comfort or discomfort level.*

Our tendency, of course, is to do whatever it takes to get rid of discomfort. Here I'm saying that in many situations it is more prudent to allow the discomfort to remain present for a while than to take the particular action that it prompts us to take. Discomfort may tell us to order dessert, for instance, but perhaps we shouldn't. The more skilful option might be to say to the discomfort, "Thanks, but no thanks," — letting go of the desire for dessert in the process, and turning our attention elsewhere. The desire and the discomfort are intimately linked, and if we really do let go of the desire, the discomfort fades away within seconds.

We must not only deal with emotions of desire, but also with emotions of aversion. Unpleasant happenings arise all too frequently in our lives, and when they do, feelings of anger, hate, grief, or fear may arise. Often, however, by the time the emotion arises, the event that triggered it is already over. The *cause* of the emotion is history. Getting into an emotionally charged stew over something in the past accomplishes nothing useful, yet we do it again and again. We repeatedly cry over spilled milk.

What does make sense in such situations is, again, to look beyond the upsetting feeling and assess its implicit message. Is the present situation threatening to my life? Is there some action that *really is* called for? I'm not saying that letting go of strong feelings is easy. It takes practice. But does any other response make sense? If the event has already happened, getting angry accomplishes nothing. Instead, we can work on letting go of our automatic tendency to exert control, and practise non-reactivity. We can practise *not* pouring time and energy into converting impulses of hurt and anger into prolonged, painful states of hurt and anger. We can, instead, bring our attention back to the immediate situation and present moment — which is where the action always is anyway. Over time, success in letting go of reactivity helps us develop the ability to respond appropriately to the need of the moment. Try it. Practise it. Get good at it. And enjoy your new-found freedom.

12

Making Death Real

I recently heard about a ninety-three-year-old woman whose doctor told her that she was dying. Upon hearing the news she became outraged at the cruelty of fate.

"Why *ME?*" she demanded to know.

Why any of us? But that's just the way it is. For ninety-three years this woman had been "unable to take in the idea of dying," as Lewis Thomas put this strange human failing. In St. Jerome's words: "Every day we are dying, and yet we fancy ourselves to be eternal."

If we could somehow manage to understand at age twenty-three or forty-three — rather than at ninety-three — that our body is absolutely guaranteed to stop functioning, and all too soon, I'm confident that our remaining years would be better for it. Each of us lives under a death sentence. And for most of us it is only when we deeply realize this that we begin to see each day as precious and begin to live our remaining time with intensity and a sense of purpose.

The younger the age at which we can put aside the delusion of personal immortality, the longer that period of intense, focused living is likely to be. A clear sense of our own eventual death is a great clarifier and adjuster of priorities. Being aware of our death makes us think about the meaning and significance of our life. It leads us to imagine ourselves at the moment of death looking back on our lives, and prompts us to ask: "Does the life I am living have the meaning I want it to have?" If we don't like the answer to that question, it is nice to still have enough time left to do something about it.

If we drop the close-up personal perspective for a moment and stand back, we can see that each human life is, in a sense, an experiment being run by the cosmic process. The details of this experiment, however, are not all determined in advance. The consciousness associated with each experiment is capable of changing the conditions and the direction of that experiment. It is possible for the human mind to revamp and refine the experimental plan, and turn our lives into more interesting, more creative, more productive experiments. Becoming deeply aware that we will die can help this to happen. Awareness of death is often one of the preludes to becoming serious about getting a meaningful life — about approaching the time that remains with a sense of purpose and direction, rather than just letting whatever happens happen.

What does it take to wake us up? What can we do to make our death become real to us? The default option is just to wait. Simply growing older eventually does it for almost everyone. Gail Sheehy noted that many people catch their first glimpse of "the dark at the end of the tunnel" when they reach their forties. But upon getting that first glimpse, many people immediately push the awareness of death out of consciousness. For them, the terror of non-existence makes death too painful to dwell upon. Still, for almost everyone the truth does manage to sink in before age ninety-three.

A big personal scare can speed up the process. Many people who have survived a life-threatening accident or illness have, as a result of that experience, redirected their lives. So have some who simply sat through a few agonizing days, waiting for the pathologist's report on a tumour biopsy, even when the tumour turned out to be benign.

The terminal illness and death of someone we know and care about — a grandparent, a parent, a friend — can also lead us to ponder our own mortality. Today, with AIDS and cancer on the rise, even relatively young people have friends who die. Faced with the impending death of someone we love, we might ask ourselves if we are up to becoming a real friend and companion to them during this final, difficult period of their life. If this is at some level appealing to you, but also frightening, why not read one or more of the excellent books now available on the role of the helper in these situations, and then decide. *Grace and Grit*,[11] by Ken Wilber, is one such book; Steven Levine's *Healing into Life and Death*[12] is another. Also, many AIDS and cancer organizations have programs designed to help would-be helpers do a good job.

Getting involved with dying people that we haven't been close to is another option. Many communities now have hospices where people with terminal illnesses can spend this last, difficult period of their life in a less-medicalized, more-homelike situation than a hospital. Some communities also provide at-home care for the terminally ill. Most of these programs welcome volunteers and have volunteer training programs.

Involvement with the dead can also make our own death more real to us. In countries like India, where open-air cremation is still practised, it is possible to see dead people first hand. In North America, except for the occasional glimpse of a cosmetic-veneered "departed one," death is kept far from the average person. There are no opportunities to practise traditional Buddhist charnel-ground meditations here, and opportunities for direct involvement with the dead are quite limited.

For a few people, however, opportunities do arise. Some years ago I had the good fortune to work awhile as a hospital orderly. I tended to the needs of terminally ill male patients (among others) and on two occasions was attending patients just at the moment of death. It was then my task to bathe the corpse and take it to the morgue. These were very powerful experiences for me. One moment there was life; the next moment there wasn't. The stark, direct nature of these personal experiences brought home the fragility of human life as nothing before ever had. I could not help being drawn into the mystery of it all.

On another occasion, I assisted at an autopsy, and the sense of mystery and wonder deepened. I recall the white-walled room, the bright lights overhead, the stainless steel table. I watched with riveted attention as the pathologist carried out his investigation. A human body lay before me, but this body was no longer a person. The life that once filled it was gone. It struck me that life was activity. Life was function. Again and again, my sense of sight had misled me. Vision had shown me a body and said, "Here is a person." Yet the things that really mattered, the person's thoughts and behaviour, were functions. Before me now was a body, a pattern of atoms. But that more important pattern — that pattern of functions, that *person* — had vanished forever.

Afterward, I went for a walk down by the harbour. I looked at the tall pine and birch trees in front of Government House. They spoke to me of the oneness of life. From one perspective I was a person, a unique pattern of functions that would hang together for a while longer. Yet I also felt part of something more fundamental, more pervasive, more enduring. Wherever life could exist, life did exist, and I felt at-one with LIFE writ large. I felt at-one with the primal *YES!* of the universe.

13

Transcending Loneliness

We've all experienced it: Primal loneliness. Existential loneliness. That deep ache and yearning which none of us wants to feel. What is loneliness, anyway? *Why* is it? And how can we best deal with it?

Loneliness exists because it helped human beings and some of our primate forebears to survive and reproduce. Reptiles and fish lay eggs and then (in most cases) leave those eggs unattended. This works because newborn reptiles and fish are able to fend for themselves immediately after hatching, and because enough eggs are laid to allow for losses to predators. As evolution progressed, animal life became more complex and began exploiting new ecological niches. These developments had their price. The young of the new, more complex, species took longer to mature, and it became necessary for parents to begin committing time to safeguarding, feeding, and rearing their young.

Like fish and reptiles, birds also lay eggs. Unlike fish and reptiles, one or both parent birds generally hang around till the eggs hatch, and then feed the hatchlings until they can manage on their own. Ordinarily, this involves the commitment of a few weeks of parental time.

Mammalian offspring also require parental care. The mother nurses them, and in most cases introduces them to at least a few survival skills. The young of small mammals mature rapidly, and like birds, are typically on their own a few weeks after birth. Large mammals — lions, horses, cows — take longer to mature, with the period of parental tending likely to be several months rather than several weeks. Still, even that period is quite brief compared with the extended period of parenting required for primate species. Chimps, gorillas, and human children take years to reach an age where they can function on their own.

With years of caring being required to raise a young human, there is obvious value in having a mate committed to that task, and in having other supportive people around. Cooperative food gathering and food sharing, group tending of offspring, and group protection against external threats are just a few of the benefits. Loneliness was one of nature's ways of inducing our ancestors to find committed mates and form such groups.

As with other biological characteristics, loneliness did not arise from any evolutionary master plan. Rather, it arose by chance and is with us today because it helped the individuals who first experienced it to survive and reproduce. It's not hard to picture what happened. All types of mammals have physical brain structures that create feelings and emotional experiences. Hunger, fear, anger, and sexual desire are perhaps the most universal of these strong feelings, but there are others too. Let's imagine that, by chance, a mammal was born with a brain which created mental discomfort every time the animal was away from others of its kind for a prolonged period. That discomfort (those feelings of *loneliness*) would have prodded the individual to return to the others. Because group living increased the probability that this animal and its offspring would survive, the genetic coding which produced the *lonely-feelings* brain design was passed on. Eventually, loneliness became a universal feature of the human species, and (we presume) of most other primate species as well.

The way we deal with the pain of loneliness is, for many of us, not very skilful. When faced with any form of distress our usual tendency is to want to get rid of it fast. Thus, in dealing with the pain of loneliness many people gravitate toward quick fixes, and some of those fixes have negative consequences. A common fix is to get into an intimate relationship, and if the distress of loneliness is disturbing enough, that might mean almost any relationship. Getting intimate does make lonely feelings go away. But as we know, in ill-starred relationships other forms of distress soon arise. A second approach is to kill the pain chemically through alcohol or some other drug. Still another is to eat the pain away. The pangs of loneliness do feel a lot like the pangs of hunger, and for some people eating lessens the distress.

To an extent greater than we might like to admit, loneliness drives the human race (including ourselves), and determines our behaviour. We humans will go to all sorts of extremes to end the pain of loneliness. We'll get into made-in-hell relationships. We'll eat. We'll drink. We'll turn to almost anything that occupies the mind and distracts us temporarily from those dreaded lonely feelings.

There are also some skilful ways of dealing with loneliness. Not all relationships are made in hell, and one positive approach is to be patient. We can put off entering an intimate relationship until we have met one of those special people with whom we can share intellectually and spiritually as well as emotionally and physically.

Another positive approach is to engage ourselves dynamically with life. In my experience, whenever my life has been characterized by fullness, purpose, and significance, loneliness has not been an issue. At such times, lonely feelings were either totally gone or had receded far into the background — making the lack of an intimate relationship quite tolerable. On the other hand, when my days have not been full, purposeful, and creative, the lonely ache was often present and strong.

Another positive approach is to get to know our lonely feelings, accept them — even make friends with them. We think we know those feelings already, but do we really? Most of us — in our hurry to get rid of them — have gotten only a distorted glimpse. The next time you feel lonely, pay close attention to the *actual feelings* that constitute the lonely state of mind. Are the sensations themselves really terrible and awful? Or do you find, when you focus on them, that they are not much different from hunger pangs or minor stomach distress?

As pains go, the physical discomfort caused by loneliness is *not* all that horrendous. Accepting it instead of trying to push it away is quite feasible. Like the hunger pangs we get when dieting, we need to see the pain of loneliness as simply one more brain-generated message. When we diet, the rational mind knows that we are not starving and that it's safe to allow hunger pangs to remain present in conscious experience. In the same way, we can quite safely coexist with the pit-of-the-stomach loneliness messages that the brain creates. They will not destroy us.

Our efforts to make peace with loneliness can also help us gain insight into how the ego works. Evolution put lonely feelings at the core of our being, but we have never accepted either the feelings or their reason for being there. All our lives **self** has resisted those feelings. I have wanted them to go away, and have sometimes done unskilful things to make them go away. Is not a mind full of wanting the chief expression of I/ego/self? Some go even further; they maintain that the wanting mind *is* the ego.

When we stop trying to get rid of lonely feelings and fully accept them, when we allow ourselves to get intimate with loneliness, we discover that this *fate worse than death* that we have been avoiding all our lives is not that at all. We discover the joy that lies beyond wanting — the joy that lies beyond ego, beyond self.

The truth of the human situation is that not one of us is separate from the cosmic process. We are all part of something large and wonderful, and while we may at times feel disconnected from the larger whole, we in fact are not. When we come to the point where we can totally accept any feelings of loneliness that may arise — and at the same time see the interconnectedness of everything — our struggle to become free and at peace is just about over.

14

Being Really Interested

We tend to think of love as an activity, as some variety of *doing for* someone else. And love sometimes is active. But love begins with awareness, with interest, and in some circumstances interest alone is the whole expression of love. In fact, one of the most important ways to be loving is simply to be totally present with the person we are with — to be intensely interested in that person and whatever he or she is communicating to us.

Alice Burkhardt was the most present person I ever met. Alice and my mother lived down the street from each other when they were little girls, and they became best friends. Their relationship continued on through the years, so when I was born, Alice became part of my life and I became part of hers. Among the high-point memories of my childhood are fun times with Alice, and from then until her death a few years ago she inspired in me the greatest admiration.

What made Alice, Alice? I'm not sure, and I regret not having explored this question more deeply with her when she was alive. She spoke once of a teenage swimming accident that almost killed her, and indicated that it had been a significant, turning-point event in her life. *Near-death experience* was not a phrase we knew back then, but in the literature today there are many reports of ego diminishment and the expanding of a person's circle of interest and concern as a result of such experiences. Perhaps Alice's swimming experience was one of these perspective-transforming near-death events.

It was clear that her father, and the teenage summers she spent working with Jane Addams at Hull House were also important influences. Alice went to the University of Wisconsin in the early 1930s and received her Master's degree in Psychology. It was there that Alice became interested in the emerging field of *recreational therapy* — the object of which is to help people get better by helping them have fun. (Imagine! And recreational therapists are paid, too.) She worked in children's hospitals in Sun Valley, Montreal, and Chicago. Later on she was Recreation Director at Bellevue Hospital's school of nursing in New York City, and got paid to help student nurses have fun.

Alice had chosen an out-of-the-ordinary career, but for those who knew Alice it was a perfect fit and made total sense. Alice was as alive as human beings come. She would have rated a perfect 10.0 on anyone's *positive-attitude* scale and another 10.0 on their *energy* scale. She honestly felt that there was no problem that couldn't be worked out somehow, and she was right there in everyone's life, helping them to refine and rethink and make things better.

Alice's most remarkable characteristic was her amazing attentiveness and presence. If she was with you, she was **WITH YOU**. More than any other person I ever met, she lived outside the confines of an ego. Her interest always bobbed about somewhere out beyond herself. To Alice, the ego and personhood of whoever she was communicating with was the immensely important thing. If that person at some point turned Alice and Alice's life into topics of discussion, Alice wouldn't hesitate to talk about herself and her personal situation. But that was not where her interest naturally gravitated. It was as if her self, her concerns, and her interest were never for very long within her own skin. They hovered instead around whoever was nearby.

What can we learn from Alice Burkhardt? For one thing she helped me to understand that love starts with interest, and in many cases ends there. We tend to think of caring as the underlying ground or base of love. But caring starts with interest. Love starts with interest. Alice's example showed me that every time we pay attention to someone, every time we really listen, we are expressing love in a concrete and very meaningful way. If we express interest, we express love. If the interest isn't there, the love isn't there. Someone who says that they love their wife or husband or child but is not deeply interested in the details of that person's life is kidding themselves. No interest, no love. Small interest, small love. Deep interest, deep love. That's just the way it is.

We often get so preoccupied with our own personal concerns that we're not really present. We're not fully there for the other person. We don't listen with total attention and interest. At other times we stop listening when we hear something we'd rather not hear — something we disagree with, or something that makes us feel uncomfortable. We interrupt at these times to put our two cents in, and to (subtly or not so subtly) shut the other person up. If only we would open our hearts in interest, listen with attention, and respond with tenderness!

Another concern is the interest we express toward the non-personal aspects of our lives — toward our work, our hobbies, our community, our world. Just what is it in life that I love? If I ask myself, "In what am I deeply interested?" and then answer that question with total honesty, I will know what I love.

Interest is also the handle on the door to knowledge. What sincerely interests us and engages our concern, we will eventually come to know. In my experience, if we develop a strong interest, the ways and means for making contact with the object of our interest somehow manage to manifest themselves. Once they appear and we make contact, the separation disappears, and this other realm becomes part of us.

15

Co-Adventuring

Many years ago someone asked me what I was looking for in an intimate partner. I blurted out, "A co-adventurer." I didn't realize at the time how appropriate my comment was.

Helen Keller said that life is either a daring adventure or nothing, and in my view she was right on the mark. Adventures are remarkable happenings, the antithesis of the routine, familiar, and old hat. Adventures involve exploration into the unknown, and embody an element of risk. They are marked by a kind of tension: excitement, enthusiasm, and eagerness for involvement on one hand, and a certain amount of apprehension and fear on the other. This is a very healthy kind of tension. The growth/exploration vector that pulls us into adventure is opposed by a security/stasis vector holding us back. Adventures happen when the pull along the growth/exploration vector exceeds the pull in the other direction and the overall decision is GO FOR IT!

At its start, every intimate relationship is a co-adventure. Getting to know one another is inherently adventurous: Dropping the façade. Running the risks that go with opening up and revealing yourself. Feeling the excitement of a new closeness. Both people actively participate in this. It is *their* adventure. Other co-adventures follow: doing new things together, going new places, and eventually moving in with each other or getting married. But what then?

Often very little, sad to say. The *play house together* adventure does not remain an adventure for long. Soon the adventurous edge disappears, the unknown becomes known, the excitement wanes. The two stop risking. Enter sameness, boredom, and dull routine. Faced with a lack of vital common focus — some sort of ongoing co-adventure — the two turn to their individual pursuits for life satisfaction. The problem lies not with individual pursuits, which are necessary and good, but with an intimate relationship devoid of zest and adventurous happenings, a primary relationship totally lacking in mutually cooked-up excitement and fun.

Co-adventuring is different. It says that whether we spend a lot of time together or relatively little, we need to do some things together that both of us find exciting — things with juice in them, adventurous things. Almost any adventure will serve as long as both people are excitedly into it. But it can't be a pretend adventure, and the enthusiasm can't be faked. The adventure must have its roots within both of them. It must connect with the needs, values, and goals of both, and must be exciting and compelling for both.

Could it be that co-adventuring is a *necessity* for a healthy relationship, not an option? Perhaps that would be going too far. Still, I've come to feel that there isn't a healthier glue for a relationship than an exciting adventure that engages both parties. Wonderful things happen if there is at least one co-adventure either being actively pursued or on the near horizon — an adventure to which they are both committed, an adventure that they share by co-living it.

The adventure itself can take a thousand forms, and needn't involve tremendous risk. There are short-term, time-limited adventures, like scouring the countryside together for old furniture to refinish. Or fixing up a house. Or moving to a new city. Or taking an extended trip together. There are also long-term co-adventures. Perhaps pursuing a career together, or starting a business, or working together to co-create a better world, a better future.

There is yet another co-adventure. It's riskier than many, but the potential benefits are great. I refer to taking the journey of personal growth together. It's risky because growth may not happen at the same rate for each. (On the other hand, that problem is even more likely to arise if only one of the pair is actively pursuing their growth.) If both partners undertake such an adventure, remain earnest, and stay committed to travelling the path of growth, then they will experience continuing excitement and a progressive deepening of their relationship. What greater adventure to share than that of becoming all you're capable of becoming?

16

Sexual Bonding: A Caveat

At some level Grandmother understood it. People involved in a sexual relationship for a while tend to become bonded to each other, regardless of how irrational the relationship might be from other perspectives. Grandmother understood that if granddaughter got involved with that ne'er-do-well boy, it would be bad news for a long time to come.

When a relationship moves from friendship to repeated or sustained physical intimacy, something happens which makes moving away from that intimacy both difficult and painful. A bond forms in intimate relationships — partly sexual, partly emotional, partly intellectual even — a connection that is extremely painful to sever. Although it involves not just sex but the whole of being intimate, sex seems to be the real glue, and for that reason I have come to call the phenomenon *sexual bonding*.

Most of us would rather be involved in an intimate relationship than not be involved in one. There are many reasons for this. For one thing, many people who live alone experience that pit-of-the-stomach ache we call loneliness, and living together stops the ache. And then there is all the mutual support and aid that intimate partners provide for each other: sharing the rent, sharing the chores, taking over when the other is sick, etc. Last, but far from least, there are all the pleasures of sex — more regularly available now than before. No wonder people tend to couple up, and once coupled, find it hard to let go of the pleasures of closeness.

Because intimacy causes these pleasures to arise, and the pain of loneliness and unwanted celibacy to go away, the bond that forms in an intimate relationship tends to be a strong one. Any threat to that bond is apt to be resisted vigorously. One type of threat is the formation of a similar bond between one's partner and someone else — a fairly common event that usually ends up causing the parties involved a great deal of suffering. People in a boring or otherwise unsatisfactory relationship often try to set up the next intimate relationship before ending the present one. The reasons are obvious: you don't have to deal with that lonely ache again, or with all the uncertainty about finding a suitable next relationship. Deception and infidelity take place, and suffering results.

In other situations the bored party doesn't really want to end the first relationship, just have a little fun on the side. The new relationship starts with a single sexual encounter, but usually doesn't end there. A one-night stand might occur without either person establishing an emotional tie, but when there is a second encounter, and a third, and sex becomes a habit, a bond almost always forms.

Now problems arise. This new partner's needs and desires understandably escalate, and there is just no way of meeting all of them and those of the original partner too. There is only one weekend per week, for instance. With whom do you share that prime time? Multiple sexual relationships tend to create conflict and suffering in the lives of at least three people — and possibly more, because an upset person often upsets others.

Another threat to the bond between intimate partners is the threat represented by the ability of either partner to sever the bond just by walking away from the relationship. It is no news these days that the pain of separation may not be willingly accepted by the party left behind. The most pain and the greatest tragedies involve intimate relationships in which one partner (or both) has a negative self-image and diminished feeling of self worth. People with low self-esteem who are involved in intimate relationships sometimes view their relationship as a one-time-only non-repeatable miracle. "How could undeserving, inferior, unattractive me have been so lucky as to find myself involved with this other person. It could never happen again in a million years." For such people the partner's intention to leave the relationship may be perceived not only as a direct threat to their well-being, but as a threat to their very existence. The threatened person may initiate strong controlling behaviours to keep the other from leaving. Verbal abuse is one control strategy. The threat of suicide, or an actual suicide attempt is another. And among males who feel threatened, physical violence against their partners is a common escalation if verbal abuse fails to control. Then, if beatings don't work, the most desperate males kill their partners, and then sometimes kill themselves. "She can't be allowed to hurt me this much," is the typical rationale.

Why didn't society tell us about sexual bonding when we were teenagers rather than just saying, "NO! Don't do it!" ??? I'm not implying that we would have been wise enough to listen back then. But just maybe if someone had laid out the hard, painful facts (as I have tried to do here) we would have been able to pick up on some danger signals a bit earlier. Perhaps we could have avoided at least a few of the many pain-filled traps.

Sex and intimacy are going to be big drivers of human behaviour for as long as our species is around. And we are going to take risks in this area as we do in others — it's part of the great adventure of life. But if we begin to see how sexual bonding works, just maybe when we're tempted to get involved in some foolishly risky situation, the big red STOP light in our heads will come on. If we see the danger, then there's at least a chance of putting on the sexual brakes before we get ourselves and others into deep difficulties. My hope is that by naming the phenomenon, focusing on it, and pointing out the incredible power of sexual bonding to influence the behaviour of those involved, that we can help ourselves, and maybe a friend or two, avoid some suffering.

One specific suggestion is to become friends before becoming lovers. In looking back over my life I realize that I rarely did this. I rarely had the patience and stamina just to wait and explore a relationship to some depth before getting sexually involved. With no sexual involvement, saying good-by (or gradually lessening the involvement) would not have caused anyone much pain. Saying good-by after a period of sexual involvement invariably did.

17

Routes to Joy

My mother was an early riser, and a cheerful one. What's more, she felt that this was appropriate behaviour for the whole family. One of my earliest memories involves being awakened in a sunshine-filled bedroom by mother standing at the foot of my bed singing *Yellow Bird*:

> Good morning little yellow bird,
> Yellow bird,
> Yellow bird,
> Good morning little yellow bird,
> How are you?

Sometimes she sang other songs, but they were all in the same *rise and shine* genre. High on her list for a couple of years was "Oh, What a Beautiful Morning" from the hit musical of the day, *Oklahoma!* These cheery songs, sung in my mother's happy, upbeat voice, had the desired effect. I came to think that waking up and starting a whole brand-new day was great stuff.

Later on in life I discovered that many people were not infused with this same sense of early morning joy. Also, it soon became clear that singing *Yellow Bird* to them just made things worse. Why is it that some people tend to be cheery in the morning and others not? What's going on here?

Despite Mother's efforts and relative success, I do not *always* bound out of bed, delighted to greet the rosy-fingered dawn — let alone a gray one. But I have looked carefully at my early-morning moods and feelings in an attempt to discover the difference between a delight-filled morning and an "Aw, yuk" one. I discovered that blah mornings were blah mornings because something was missing. That something was *joy*. Blah mornings were joyless mornings.

Where did the joy come from on those other, more upbeat days? And is there a route to joy, a way to find that mental space more reliably? One thing I noticed was that whenever I had something to look forward to — some fun or meaningful element in the day ahead, something enjoyable — the joy was also there when the day began. Some sort of inspiring daily activity, then, is one route to joy, and we could take the approach of trying to put at least one enjoyable activity into the structure of each coming day. We could make an effort beforehand to set up something to look forward to.

I recall a difficult time in my life when I used this approach. A demanding family situation was threatening to drain the joy from every moment, but something deep within said, "No, I'm not going to let that happen." My way of finding enjoyment was to get up each morning an hour before the rest of the family. That hour was mine alone, to devote to my projects, to activities that excited me and put me in a joyous state of mind. Waking up at 5 a.m. became a special treat, the entrée to an hour of fun. And the joy which arose during that hour lingered on, helping me deal with the more demanding aspects of the day.

Even our daily work can sometimes be structured so that anticipation and excitement draw us joyfully into it. Some writers use the trick of stopping their day's writing in the middle of something interesting, and leaving it unfinished. The interesting unfinished task then becomes the bait that draws the writer enthusiastically into the next day's writing. Even if your work seems totally devoid of interest, perhaps you could work something enlivening into your lunch break: Lunch with a friend? Reading the book you've been eager to start? Listening to that new tape?

Sometimes restructuring our time is impossible; we simply can't modify existing activities or squeeze in new ones. *Appreciation*, however, is never ruled out, and appreciating life is a second route to joy. Can we reactivate our appreciation of each moment? Perhaps we could take a few moments each morning to consciously affirm our good fortune at being alive. When we can bring ourselves to appreciate another day of living in this wondrous universe, joy just naturally arises. The task is to recapture that sense of wide-eyed excitement we all experienced at age four. Since we are still continuously surrounded by the marvellous and wondrous it shouldn't be hard, but it often seems to be. Sometimes it takes a brush with death to awaken us from the deadness of inattention and undervaluation. Sometimes an encounter with some new-to-us aspect of nature does it — discovering, right before us, some little miracle that we never before noticed. Perhaps it's time simply to stop — then look, listen, and wonder. Opening up to wonder can bring us joy.

A third route to joy is to practise smiling. Long advocated by some spiritual teachers, scientific research recently confirmed that this practice really works. We have always known that when we feel joy it tends to make us smile. But it is also true that if we smile, it tends to make us feel joyous. Try it. Consciously smile your way through a day or two, and see if it doesn't lift your spirits.

There is one more route to joy. It is the most radical way, and the least often pursued. Yet it is the most direct, most basic way. This way comes out of insight into the nature of joy itself. This fourth way to find joy is to realize that joy is part of the ground of life, and just practise being joyful.

Joy, it turns out, does not require any external cause at all. It is Joseph Campbell's *bliss* — naturally there when our lives are on track, perpetually present when not displaced by distress or boredom. It is the primal *Ananda* of Brahman. It is Chogyam Trungpa's *Basic Goodness*. It is the natural mental space of babies and young children when they are not distressed. Joy is experienced whenever we stop getting distracted from, and stop interfering with, the experience. Joy is experienced whenever the mind becomes quiet and drops its wanting, craving, rejecting, condemning ways. Joy is experienced whenever we allow it to be experienced.

18

Rediscovering Wonder

How often do you find yourself lost in wonder? Frequently? Rarely? Or does the whole idea of wonder seem silly and childish to you?

There is something childlike about wonder, and wonder seems to arise quite frequently and naturally in childhood. Of my own moments of wonder, the first that I clearly remember occurred during the summer of 1941. I was five years old then, and my father had just given me a crystal set radio and a pair of *Cannonball* headphones — earphones we called them back then.

There wasn't much to the crystal set. The base was a piece of one-eighth-inch-thick hardboard about seven inches square. At the back of the board was a coil of fine wire about the size of a toilet paper tube. Just in front of the coil was the crystal — a small piece of shiny *galena* lead ore embedded in a cylinder of soft metal. Right next to the crystal was a curious assembly known as a *cat's whisker*. It allowed a stiff, springy wire to be brought into contact with any desired point on the crystal's surface.

My father was excited, I could see that, and his excitement was infectious. I sensed that this was neat stuff, and was eager to try the little radio. Not yet, my father explained. Although the crystal set didn't need electricity to make it work, it did need a high-up wire antenna and a *ground* connection.

My father discovered that someone, years before, had installed an antenna in the attic. He connected a new lead-in wire to the old antenna, dropped it out the attic window, and brought it through another window into my bedroom. He then attached that wire and a wire from a radiator to spring clips on the crystal set. He put the earphones on and slowly and carefully moved the cat's whisker around on the crystal. When he finally found the sought-for "hot" spot, his face turned into one big smile. Continuing to grin, he took the earphones off his head, adjusted the headband so they'd fit me, and slipped them on my ears.

I couldn't believe it. Music! In my head! From somewhere! All this magic from a board, a coil, and a crystal. How could it be? It was wonderful. Dad told me that the antenna picked up radio signals from the air, and something that amazing seemed to be happening — but how? This was something special, something out-of-the-ordinary, something miraculous.

This sort of radio-inspired wonder continued to surface from time to time as I grew up. I can remember sitting at a card table with my father a year and a half later as he put together a two-tube earphone radio for me. Then, when I was nine, while poring over a library book on radio, I came to a chapter that described this very same radio — MY radio. I read that if I only had a set of four-prong, short-wave plug-in coils for it, I could listen to stations from other countries. WOW!

Dad to the rescue again. We went down to New York's Cortlandt Street — roughly where the World Trade Center is now — and bought a set of plug-in coils. That night I listened to the BBC and Radio Moscow ... wonder, wonder, and more WONDER! Later, in my teens, I became a ham radio operator. Time and time again the wonder arose anew as I conversed with people half a world away by means of magical signals from equipment sitting in front of me that I had built myself.

My childhood interest in radio eventually led me to enter engineering school, and through my studies much about the world around me became demystified; a lot of the magic was rendered rational. Despite this, the wonder didn't disappear. Even today when I sit at my ham radio set and talk to someone in Europe, or the Caribbean, or the South Pacific, or exchange on-the-air pictures or keyboard data with them, that feeling of wonder arises again.

Rather than destroying wonder for me, my knowledge of science redirected it. Again and again, technology had prompted experiences of wonder, but over the years the wonder became not so much a response to a technology as to the underlying natural order which allowed that technology to function. Science explains the details of our world; it makes the specifics rational. Science tells me, for instance, that under certain circumstances, with the right equipment, I *should* be able to talk to people around the world. The laws of nature allow it to happen — no, they *insist* on it happening. When science makes the manifest details rational in this way, the wonder moves down a level, to the existence of a universe that allows such happenings. *Everything* becomes wondrous, sacred. Whence came these marvellous laws of nature that permit rational magic? I don't know, but I am wonderstruck by the fact that existence is the way it is. Nature itself is the GREAT WONDER, and the source of all the specific wonders.

Many people who might not see wonder in scientific law find it in direct encounters with the natural world. Thoreau lets us feel this:

> We need the tonic of wildness — to wade sometimes in marshes where the bittern and the meadow-hen lurk, and hear the blooming of the snipe; to smell the whispering sedge where only some wilder and more solitary fowl builds her nest, and the mink crawls with its belly close to the ground.[13]

> As I come over the hill, I hear the wood thrush singing his evening lay. This is the only bird whose note affects me like music, affects the flow and tenor of my thought, my fancy and imagination. It lifts and exhilarates me. It is inspiring. It is a medicative draught to my soul. It is an elixir to my eyes and a fountain of youth to all my senses. It changes all hours to an eternal morning.[14]

And in his way, Whitman, too, takes us there:

As to me I know of nothing else but miracles,
Whether I walk the streets of Manhattan,
Or dart my sight over the roofs of houses toward
    the sky,
Or wade with naked feet along the beach just in
    the edge of the water,
Or stand under trees in the woods,

. . . .

Or watch honey-bees busy around the hive of a
    summer forenoon,
Or animals feeding in the fields,
Or birds, or the wonderfulness of insects in the
    air,
Or the wonderfulness of the sundown, or of stars
    shining quiet and bright,
Or the exquisite delicate thin curve of the new
    moon in spring;
These with the rest, one and all, are to me
    miracles, …[15]

What can we do to experience wonder more frequently? Recapturing a childlike orientation to experience is one thing, and we could probably all benefit from hanging out with pre-schoolers, nine-year-olds, and turned-on teens. There are other approaches, too. The most popular one in our culture is to intentionally put ourselves in some intense, awesome, or mind-boggling situation. Who could view Arizona's Grand Canyon without experiencing wonder? Or watch the birth of a baby? Or, as I described back in chapter 12, assist at an autopsy?

There is a third way of bringing wonder into our lives: quiet our minds. The busyness of the world around us and the busyness of our individual lives distance us from wonder. Powerful new experiences — like visiting the Grand Canyon or seeing a baby born — override this ordinary-life noise level, and may wake us up to wonder. But there is wonder all around us, all the time, and quieting the mind allows us to see the wonder in a flower, an insect, a person's touch. So while powerful experiences trigger episodes of wonder, a quiet mind lets us live with wonder more continuously. A new kind of pleasure becomes available to us.

There are various ways of quieting the mind. Spending a week or two alone somewhere without books or electronic media is one way. Attending a seven- or ten-day silent meditation retreat is another. Unfortunately, when someone first goes from the buzzing world into solitude and quiet circumstances they often perceive it as a negative change. Most of us are accustomed to high-level stimulation, and when that stimulation stops, our initial reaction is one of deprivation. We want it to start up again. Because we have become desensitized by the bash and buzz and wail of modern life, when we do enter the quiet, things for a time seem distant, indistinct, and out of reach. If we are willing to put up with this uneasy state for two or three days, it passes. Isolated from noise, from artificially set up pleasure hits, and other high-level inputs, our senses slowly, gradually, regain their natural sensitivity. After a week or two of solitude and quiet, the simple life becomes positively full — filled by the countless stimuli of the everyday world. We then begin to see the wondrous world which our battered, bruised, overstimulated senses have been neglecting. The world of Thoreau and Whitman is still there for any of us who want badly enough to enter it.

19

Enhancing Creativity

Being deeply involved in creative activity is one of the most enjoyable experiences we human beings can have. What's more, it allows us to put something back into the pot of life, to give something of value to others. For many people, though, creativity seems mysterious and out of reach — a gift given to some people and not to others. The truth is that it is not a rare gift, but a quite understandable process — one that any of us can use to enhance our enjoyment of life.

Different writers have different views about what creativity is, and about how the creative process works. Some make distinctions between different kinds of creativity. Here I address two kinds:

- One is production-related creativity: *the production of something novel or unique that has value.*
- The other is discovery-related creativity: *the discovery, through human insight, of some new fact, law, or feature of the world.*

By production-related creativity I don't mean just novel inventions and product designs, though that is part of it. I mean the creation of something of value that never existed before, in *any* creative medium: canvas and paint, clay, bronze, electronics, architectural materials, machined metal, welded metal, words, biochemistry, and a hundred others. The product or creation need not be novel in all respects, but something about it must be unique, and it must have value — aesthetic value, utilitarian value, inspirational value, or value of some other kind.

Discovery-related creativity is a little harder to pin down. Central to it is human insight, the seeing of something in a uniquely different (or at least highly unusual) way. One of its manifestations is the scientific breakthrough where insight leads to yet another layer being peeled off the onion of truth. Another manifestation of discovery-related creativity is spiritual seeing, where the individual flips to a new and more helpful perspective on things — to a superior way of interpreting the data of reality. The task of expressing these insights of discovery to others involves a return once again to production-related creativity. How does one share what one has seen?

Author Robert Weisberg[16] feels that creativity arises from quite ordinary thought processes at times when those processes are being pursued deeply and intensely. For him, creativity is simply what you get when you mix expertise in some *domain* (area of activity or investigation) with a lot of motivation and commitment.

I agree that expertise, motivation, and commitment are essential and that they sometimes do lead directly to creative products and discoveries. But in my experience, the process of bringing forth valuable novelty often differs from business-as-usual thinking and problem solving. The four-stage creative process outlined some years ago by Graham Wallas[17] fits my experience quite closely. Wallas's four stages are:

1. **Preparation.**
2. **Incubation.**
3. **Illumination.**
4. **Verification.**

I will share my thoughts about each of these, and will share a few observations from others.

Preparation means preparation in two senses. The first sense involves the need to develop, over time, the basic skills and expertise that one must have to function creatively in the particular domain. If electronics is your medium, and you want to design new kinds of electronic equipment, you must first learn a great deal about the medium itself and the principles behind the functioning of electronic components and circuits. If you want to do unique things with paint and canvas, the preparation can be just as arduous. The medium itself is simpler, but you will probably need to explore and master a great many ways of using it before you will be able to creatively *step beyond* what has gone before.

Howard Gardner[18] speaks to this general kind of preparation with his observation that if highly creative things are going to happen in a person's life, they often happen about ten years into a career. To be innovative in any field you have to have done your homework and paid your dues; there doesn't seem to be any way around that. Creativity builds on, and takes off from, what has gone before. It takes time to assimilate *what* has been done by others, *how* they did it, and *why*. It also takes time to become skilled in the techniques and technology of a creative medium, be it music, art, electronics, sewing, or scientific research.

In the information processing view of mind, creativity is a data processing activity that produces its results through the manipulation of available data. In this view, the more data there is to process, the greater will be the likelihood of an output emerging that is both novel and useful. Thus, we would expect an investigative attitude and rich life experience to enhance creativity. I have also noticed that my creativity tends to be cyclical. Periods of creating/outputting/giving usually alternate with periods of learning/inputting/growing.

The second kind of preparation, the situation-specific kind, involves a period of intense mental activity. If there is a problem to be solved, you

- **define the problem** (ideally in the broadest possible way, or perhaps in several different ways),
- **gather information** (information that bears on this problem and on how similar problems have been solved in the past), and

- **actively try to think, feel, or see your way to a solution.** (The specifics depend on the nature of the creative problem. You might visualize physical situations; draw diagrams; solve equations; do trial and error things with a musical or computer keyboard; or try lateral thinking, brainstorming, or some other perspective-shifting technique.)

If gathering information and wrestling with the problem in this way does not yield a solution, it may mean that you need still more information. Or it may mean that it is time to move on to the next stage of the process.

Incubation is the next stage, and it involves taking time out from the problem. The theory is that while your conscious mind takes a rest from active work on the problem, your subconscious still works behind the scenes to find a solution. And again and again, that does seem to happen. Pieces of the puzzle that you might not have consciously thought about during active preparation sometimes come together during this period. It is as though the intense work in the preparation phase has activated all your mental capabilities, including subconscious ones, and the search for a creative breakthrough continues in some unconscious brain process.

Illumination, when it follows incubation, usually arrives as a flash of insight — the famous Aha! or Eureka! experience. What comes might not be the complete answer. Rather, it might be part of the answer, or perhaps just a clue about where to find the answer.

Verification, the final stage of the process, involves either intellectually fleshing out the illumination in detail, or testing its practicality. In some situations you might create a model, a sketch, a "breadboard" circuit, or in the case of a work of art, the work itself. Some of the time this verification process is trivially simple; at other times it involves a great deal of work.

There are a few things about creativity that I'd like to stress. For one thing, my years in electronics taught me that to be creative you must become familiar with the *current state of the art*. You need to know, in other words, what has been done before. There is no point reinventing the wheel, as the saying goes. And while one's ego wants to believe that it is capable of bringing forth something exciting and novel out of an informationless vacuum, reality doesn't work that way. Creativity, I have come to see, is almost always a *next step* or *step beyond* process. It was that even for Einstein — though his steps were giant steps.

I also want to share with you my observation that quieting our minds can lead to more creativity in all aspects of life. There is both *great creativity* and *everyday creativity*, and those lives which have creativity woven into their very structure are rewarding lives indeed. Problem-oriented creativity is often facilitated by an intense desire for a solution and much hard work. If we work intensely on some creative problem — writing a book, creating a piece of sculpture, designing a piece of electronic equipment, or finding out something about how the universe works — the very intensity of the creative effort helps creative insights to break through the barrier between conscious and subconscious mental processes. In other words, a high-intensity, pressure-cooker milieu facilitates the process.

Paradoxically, a quiet mind also facilitates the creative process. And interestingly, whereas high intensity preparation only applies to the solving of well-defined creative problems, a quiet mind facilitates every kind of creativity. Returning to the barrier metaphor, high intensity seems to force insights through the barrier while a quiet mind works by thinning the barrier out, by making it more permeable.

It is difficult in the workaday world to cultivate mental quiet, but it is not impossible. Some people sit quietly and meditate once or twice a day. A related approach is to return our attention to immediate circumstances during those pauses in life when we usually space out, fantasize, plan, or reminisce. Standing in line, sitting in the dentist's waiting room, and waiting for a red light to change are all opportunities to drop discursive thought and just pay attention. Other approaches are Yoga; Tai Chi; various sports; prolonged meditation in a retreat environment;[19] and as mentioned previously, spending time alone without books, magazines, radio, TV, or music. Again, one of the nice things about quieting your mind is that it facilitates the everyday kind of creativity as well as great creativity. A quiet mind often leads to useful insights even when you have no specific "creative problem" to work on.

Many writers, artists, and other creative people intentionally choose living and working arrangements that provide long periods of solitude and relative freedom from distractions. They know that they are more creative when their minds are relatively quiet. They understand that it is important for the intellect and the non-verbal, subconscious processes to work together, and they know that this happens most effectively in quiet circumstances.

For a long time it has been common for artists and writers to attribute any genius they might have to *The Muse*. They have held that this non-intellectual, other-than-them *something* is the source of all their good, really creative stuff. Today we know *The Muse* to be these unconscious mental processes that work on behalf of the intellect to solve our creative problems for us and make our creative breakthroughs. Working intently in the preparation stage of the process is one way to help establish a creative partnership between the intellect and *The Muse*. Quieting our noisy, left-brain, thinking mind is another. I highly recommend both.

20

Real Happiness

Finding lasting happiness. Becoming a joyous, loving person. Attaining peace of mind. These are universal human aspirations, and are not terribly far out of reach. The truth is that **happiness, quiet joy, love, and peace exist when reactivity is absent.** Awareness, contentment, freedom, and love are aspects of the primal, underlying state of mind — a state which simply *is*. Unhappiness is a disturbance of that state, a disruptive modulation of it. Unhappiness is a wanting, judging, condemning, rejecting, emotionally charged reaction to information that is present in the mind.

One of our culture's strong messages is that happiness comes from satisfying our wants — from taking seriously, and acting upon, the messages of desire and longing and wanting that arise in consciousness. Our culture tells us that happiness comes from pleasure, and if we want to be continuously happy, we should spend time setting up a continuous series of pleasure hits.

There is, however, another perspective on happiness. Those with this other point of view say that there is no need to *seek* happiness, happiness simply *is* when mental reactivity is not. Thus, the task is not to become happy; it is to stop making ourselves unhappy. These people point out that the storms of reactive emotion we call *fear, anger, hate* and *craving* — all of them ways of wanting things to be different — are what disturb the otherwise smooth ocean of peaceful awareness that is happiness itself.

If we want to live a life of inner peace and outwardly directed love we need to do two things. First, we need to give up the hopeless task of trying to make the world immediately around us so pleasant that unwanted mind content never arises. Second, when unhappy disturbances first arise in the mind we need to avoid feeding energy into them. In nature, if energy continues to enter the modest *tropical disturbance* type of storm, it will become a hurricane. It is the same with storms of reactive emotion. An impulse of fear, anger, hate, or craving may arise in the mind, totally beyond our control. If at that point we just note the impulse and let it go, it never becomes a mind-dominating tempest. On the other hand, if we feed energy into the situation by creating a story to go with the feelings, those feelings are likely to escalate from a puny pang of discomfort into a mental hurricane.

We don't ignore the emotion-tinged messages that arise in the mind or deny their existence, but neither do we assume that we must dwell on them or act on them. We don't need to let them spoil our day. While some messages do need to be taken seriously and acted upon, many others advocate action that is inappropriate in present circumstances. If we let the feelings remain without reacting to them — allowing them to stay, simply as messages on the notice-board of mind — they soon fade completely away.

Separating the kind of message that should be acted upon from the kind that should be ignored requires attention and discrimination. We humans have certain basic needs which only the world around us can meet. Each of us needs food, housing, some degree of security, and supportive relationships with other people. As Abraham Maslow saw it, if our immediate environment doesn't give us these things we cannot be whole, well, human beings.

The Gautama Buddha was a strong proponent of the inward-looking perspective, but he, too, recognized that we have needs which must be met through external resources. He advocated a *middle path* between the extremes of deprivation and indulgence. You turn to the physical situation to meet your needs, but not to satisfy your greed. On the middle path, you don't starve yourself or freeze yourself. You approach the external world to get the food and shelter you need to keep you healthy. And you approach it to find a community of supportive people — within which your needs for belongingness and psychological/spiritual growth can be met.

If trying to change our physical situation sometimes makes sense, and accepting *what is* sometimes makes sense, where do we draw the line?

The Protestant theologian Reinhold Niebuhr acknowledged the difficulty and defined the problem in his famous prayer:

> … give us serenity to accept what cannot be changed,
> courage to change what should be changed, and wis-
> dom to distinguish one from the other.[20]

Not everyone would draw the line exactly where Niebuhr drew it. The version of Niebuhr's prayer adopted by Alcoholics Anonymous, for example, uses the words "change the things I *can*" rather than "change what *should* be changed." The AA version is oriented more to the capability of the individual to change things; Niebuhr's more to the demand for change inherent in the situation itself.

Some proponents of acceptance — particularly those concerned about our fragile biosphere — would advocate less change than either Niebuhr or AA advocated. They might prefer something like: "Accept what cannot *or should not* be changed."

There are many things we cannot change — ageing and death for example. Each of us who doesn't die young will eventually grow old and deteriorate physically. A biologist acquaintance expressed it with brutal directness: "Every living thing is programmed to self-destruct." We all understand this intellectually. Nevertheless, many people maintain an externally oriented mindset as they approach old age, irrationally hoping that reality for them will be different. To the very end they direct their energy and attention outward, pinning their hopes for peace of mind and happiness on the success of external measures — measures which, at some point, are guaranteed to fail. It doesn't occur to them to channel some of that energy and attention into discovering how to handle, with equanimity, whatever old age might throw their way.

Yes, we humans fall into traps. North American culture strongly supports the trap of perpetual, narcissistic, pleasure seeking. Its repetitive message is: **find happiness by satisfying your wants**. Sometimes, wants and needs coincide. Our world is full of legitimate, unmet basic needs, and there is every reason to take personal and collective action to help people meet them. But the consumer culture's core message is *not* that we should help others, it's that we should satisfy our own wants. Pleasure is its guiding value, and consumption is its recommended way. This culture does a great job of preparing us to function, to act, to acquire, to change things. It does not prepare us to accept what we cannot, should not, and need not change. It does not teach us to allow the actions we take to be guided from a quiet centre of concern and interest. It does not do much to help us become wise.

The inward-looking path has its traps, too. One of these is maintaining a preoccupation with self, and losing oneself in narcissism. In this circumstance, too, pleasure remains the guiding value, and consumption (in somewhat subtler forms) remains the way. People trapped here miss the deeper point of their chosen practice of inner development, and end up becoming attached to its techniques. They may take pride in the length of their meditation sittings, for instance, and the number and duration of the retreats they attend. They want to "have" spiritual experiences. As a result, egos harden rather than dissolve.[21]

Developing the ability to accept whatever *is*, non-reactively, does not mean that we abandon positive kinds of action. Ideally, we return from silence and retreat to participate actively in the world, but with a more spacious, more allowing, more enlightened mental outlook.

Acquiring an enlightened outlook is not apt to happen in a weekend. Part of the reason is that we lack facts and we harbour well-entrenched delusions. We lack facts, for instance, in the area of brain/mind functioning. And a major delusion is the one we just looked at: We tend to blame our personal unhappiness on externals, and see only one path to happiness. We feel that we must change the external situation in some way — through direct action, appeal to reason, coercion, manipulation, or force — until it matches our expectations, until it gives us what we want.

What we can do about our unenlightened state is to start gathering missing facts, and start taking those steps which will ultimately allow us to see through the delusions. We can learn enough about the processes of mind and brain to discover the rules of the happiness/peace/love game. We can discover where our points of leverage lie in dealing with the unruly aspects of mind, and we can develop those ways of being which enable us to acknowledge mind's informational patterns without generating reactive storms. Finally, we can pay attention to our own experience of happiness and unhappiness, and draw our own conclusions about what they are. In the end, we see for ourselves that real happiness is simply freedom from wanting.[22]

21

Opening the Heart

Is it possible to develop a compassionate concern about every person, the rest of life on earth, and about the whole process and all its expressions? I'm convinced that it is, and will discuss three of the many possible ways of working our way to that place of caring and compassion.

One way to develop a compassionate attitude toward people is through coming to appreciate the lawfulness of the universe and the human decision-making process. There are reasons why things happen, and deeply understanding this enables us to see that no matter how unskilful a person's actions are, at the moment of decision that person is doing the best they can.

We live in a lawful universe. At any given instant a certain situation exists, and that situation interacts with the laws of nature — and sometimes with the decision-making systems of people and animals — to produce a new situation in the next instant. What happens does not have just one single cause. Instead, multiple elements in each situation *together* dictate what will happen. Any single "cause" that we might identify is linked to other causal factors in the situation, and each of those has causes of its own. What we have are countless chains of cause and effect that go all the way back to the beginning of our universe fifteen billion years ago. The effects of chance and randomness in forging some of the links in those chains do nothing to change this picture. There is no single cause for anything. Things happen exactly as they happen at this moment because a near infinitude of other things happened exactly as they happened at times in the past, and resulted in the present multifaceted situation.

Our individual brains and our decision-making capabilities came out of this complex causal matrix, and as much as we might like to think of ourselves as self-made and independent-minded, we are in fact, universe made. Each person's actions are determined by a complex, decision-making system that is itself the result of a multitude of causal influences. The residual effects of these influences now determine how decisions will be made and what they will be.

Helping to form this system and determine how it operates are

- the genes we ended up with after billions of years of biological evolution,
- our local and global cultures,
- the family we grew up in,
- the schools we attended,
- the friends we hung out with,
- the TV and movies we have watched, and
- the books, magazines, and newspapers we have read.

These and other influences helped form the individualized decision-making systems that decide what we will do and what we won't do in various circumstances. It is these brain-based systems that decide, out of zillions of possibilities, the particular actions we take — and in concert with many things that we have no control over, the lives we end up living.

Essential to the decision-making process are what we call our *values.* Human decision-making involves a whole hierarchy of these values, and one thing we can be sure of is that your value hierarchy will be different from mine. Even if you and I agree on broad general principles, we will disagree on details. And even in the extremely unlikely event that we had exactly the same list of values, my decision-making system would probably not rank their relative importance in the same way that yours would. Because of this, in identical situations you and I would often make different decisions.

So just how does this work in real life? Feeding the birds is one of my values, but it ordinarily has a much lower priority than feeding myself. Thus, if I'm down to my last dollar I'm much more likely to buy myself a hamburger than to spend it on bird seed. Down to your last dollar, something else might happen. Feeding the birds might not be on your list at all, and perhaps you don't eat meat. In some way not yet understood in detail, both our present situation and the hierarchy of values that each of us has internalized are taken into account. Then, out of the myriad of possible actions, our decision-making process decides to take one of them — or perhaps decides to do nothing.

One of the things we can deduce from this decision-making reality is that **everyone is doing the best they can**. A person has made a decision. Perhaps if he or she had possessed a little more information, or slightly different information, the decision made might have been very different. But at the instant of decision, the decision itself could not have been anything other than what it was.

We may not understand why a particular decision was made, nor understand how it could possibly have been the optimum choice of any conceivable decision-making system. But just because we don't understand the rationale does not mean that there was none. At some deeper level, beyond our understanding, everything that happens makes sense. The combined personal/cosmic system took into account everything pertaining to that situation — including the design and programing of the human brain that made the decision. And out of the whole matrix of interrelated elements came a decision and a happening that was the logical consequence of all those elements and their relationship.

If, as this indicates, everyone is doing the best they can, how then can we feel anything other that compassion for everyone? I'm not saying that we should tell the rapist or the drive-by killer that we're so sorry about their problem, and let them run free. Destructive people can't be allowed to continue to destroy; it's as simple as that. But at the same time we must realize that some combination of influences came together to form the decision-making systems that got these people to do what they did. We can then try to figure out what those influences were, and do our best to see that others are not subjected to them.

111

OPENING THE HEART

Let's assume that this sort of analysis brings us to a *rational* understanding that people are doing the best they can, but toward many people we still don't *feel* compassionate. What can we do about that?

One possibility is to start extending caring feelings to others, and to do this repeatedly. Buddhists call the extending of good wishes to others *lovingkindness meditation.* You simply sit comfortably in a quiet place and extend wishes for happiness and well-being to yourself and others. You begin with the easiest situation. If you like yourself, then you start by wishing yourself happiness and well being. In Asian cultures, this is where almost everyone starts. In North America, however, many people find wishing themselves happiness more difficult than wishing others happiness. In this case, start with a person that you admire a great deal and leave yourself till later — perhaps even till last.

When wishing happiness and well-being to this first person has a comfortable feel to it, you then extend the same sort of good wishes to other "easy" people — people who you admire — one person at a time.

When, after some practise, doing this for people you like feels right and comfortable, you are encouraged to start selecting various "difficult" people — people who have hurt you, perhaps, or other people to whom sending good wishes is not so easy. You move into this "difficult" area only to the extent that you are drawn to do so. But most people find that as they practise wishing people the best that life has to offer, they are eventually able to extend their circle of care and concern to difficult people, and ultimately to everyone.

As I see this practice, whether or not your good wishes do these other people any good is beside the point. The object is to do YOU some good — to help you feel more connected with others — more understanding, more compassionate.

On a related matter, what is your typical reaction when someone tells you about an award they just received, or a trip they are about to take to a wonderful place, or some other piece of personal good fortune? Is it a twinge of envy? Or is it genuine excitement for them, and a feeling of gladness on their behalf? We all know what envy is, but this other state of mind has a name, too. It's called *sympathetic joy*, and it's envy's opposite. Again, if our tendency is to feel envy at the good fortune of others, we can work to change that situation by practising sympathetic joy.

Another way to arrive at a place of universal compassionate concern is to come to understand what oneness means, and to start to feel the connectedness that already exists among all forms of life, and between life forms and the rest of the universal process. This approach was advocated by the mystics and spiritual teachers of ancient times. The challenge is to see through the temporary realm of form and appearance to the enduring realm of Being that supports form and appearance, and is their source.

"Energy cannot be created or destroyed, but only changed in form." That is what our high school physics teachers told us, and they were right. I think that the enduring substrate of the universe which the ancients called *Being* is the same enduring reality that we today call energy — or more correctly, energy in concert with the laws by which it functions. What the ancients called *form* we today call *information*: patterns of difference in some medium of expression. Energy interpenetrates everything in the physical world and allows it to exist. Energy is the medium, or carrier, or beingness of the entire universe. Information gives form to the energy. Every **thing** is an informational elaboration of energy. In fact, we can look at all existence as information-patterned energy. The information constantly changes in response to the dictates of the laws of nature, and human and animal decision making, but the stuff that lasts — the *energy* itself — never changes. Energy just *is*.

Most of us have trouble seeing reality this way because our sense of what is real and not real is so very strongly influenced by our sense of vision. Vision misleads us in two ways. First, it tells us things that are not true. Vision tells us that the world is full of solid, separate *things*, even though so-called solids are more than 99.9 per cent empty space, and even though visual boundaries may not be boundaries at all from other perspectives. For instance, vision reinforces the belief that we are independent people, separate from everything else. This just isn't true. (Think about our intimate connection with the atmosphere, for instance.) This *thingness* problem is compounded by our subject-verb-object language which tends to reinforce vision's chopped-up slant on reality.

The second problem with vision is that it fails to reveal to us some important things that are true. Vision does not reveal to us either the underlying oneness, or the labyrinth of connections and links between various aspects of the process. Energy is real, all would agree, but it is not a **thing**, and it is not visible. And as for those interconnections, most are not visually obvious. Think again about our connection with the atmosphere; if it ceased to exist, we'd die in a real hurry. But because air is transparent, vision (our primary tool for making sense of the world around us) fails to report its presence. The old saying, "out of sight, out of mind" seems to be literally true.

The way evolution works, any new chance-created features that help a species survive and reproduce tend to be passed on genetically to future generations. We human beings inherited a way of seeing that helped us to survive in the circumstances we faced a hundred thousand years ago. And the human visual system continues to help us deal effectively with a multitude of everyday situations. But when we try to comprehend reality-writ-large, vision misleads us badly in the ways just mentioned.

"How could evolution have let this happen?" you ask. "Isn't evolution constantly refining and improving?"

Evolution tends to weed out errors in a living being's understanding of reality *if those errors have a strong negative impact on survival or reproduction.* But evolution can also promote and maintain errors in understanding if those errors *enhance* survival and reproduction.

In my book *TOWARD WISDOM,* I take the position that the strong sense of personal identity that almost every human being possesses is just such an error. From a rational, scientific perspective we are not independent beings, we are subsystems of a much larger system that includes at least the sun, geological earth, atmosphere, and biosphere. That is hard-nosed scientific fact. **From a strictly rational perspective it makes more sense to identify with the system as a whole than with this highly dependent subsystem of the whole called a human being.**

If we could see the world through the perceptual systems of a frog or a lobster or an insect, we would no doubt be appalled at the more distorted and limited view of reality that these creatures have compared with ours. Yet these species have been around for a long time — much longer than human beings. Their perceptual and cognitive data processing systems *meet their survival and reproduction needs*, and so have continued to exist, despite failing to "tell it like it is" according to some objective standard of truth.

Our brain-mind systems were designed for survival and reproduction in a hunter-gatherer environment — an environment that was often characterized by scarcity, low or no technology, and by multiple dangers to life. Picture two of our ancestors 20,000 years ago. Let's imagine that the first person happened to have a visual system and brain that allowed her to see the larger pattern of connections, and which induced her to identify with the system as a whole rather than with body and mind contents. And let's imagine that the second person had normal vision and a brain that made sense of things in the usual personal-identity way. In the world that then existed, which perspective would have had greater survival value? I strongly suspect it would have been the personal perspective. In a world of limited resources and immediate dangers, person-centred concern has survival value, whereas concern about the whole does not. Evolution selected out and passed on a mentality that viewed things erroneously because that erroneous view gave the human being who possessed it a distinct survival and reproduction advantage under the difficult conditions that then existed.

That environment existed from the time humans first evolved until agriculture began about seven thousand years ago. Geneticists would tell us that our genes have not changed much in the past seven thousand years. It is the human situation that has changed. Only with the arrival of the industrial revolution did the personal-identity error start to become counterproductive, and only during our present century — when human powers were expanded immensely by technology — did it become a danger to species survival.

As many others have pointed out, the pursuit of personal comfort and pleasure by billions of technology-controlling, person-centred minds fast depletes global resources and mucks up the global environment. Today the situation is very different from that of 100,000 years ago, and **in our present circumstances it is identification with the whole that has survival value.** Continuing to identify as persons threatens to destroy us all.

To summarize, there is only one enduring reality. It is the oneness that the mystics spoke about, and that oneness is our deepest, truest identity. In ancient times it was called Being. Today we have other names for it. Physically, we call it *energy*. Mentally, we call it *awareness*. In one or both of these guises it is present within and around us. In the physical world energy acquires various forms — various informational mouldings or shapings. In our brains there is a patterned firing of neurons, and those neuronal energy discharges modulate awareness to create that other kind of informational pattern we call mind content.

The task is to *see through* the informational modulations of matter and mind to the enduring reality that underlies, supports, and "carries" those modulations. In seeing through the busyness of informational appearances — seeing through everything we see, hear, taste, smell, touch, and think — we can apprehend this fundamental oneness, and recognize it as our deepest, truest nature. If we cultivate this alternative perspective and succeed in making it our own, we find that the differentiation between *self* and *other* retreats from its usual dominant position. Instead of being up front, always in our face, the you/me difference recedes into the background. Remaining in the foreground is only *the situation*, and whatever the wisdom within prompts us to do about the situation. Compassion is present because *everything* is included in this expanded sense of self, and because we see that every person and other aspect of the process is universe doing its best — no matter how unskilful or immoral that best may be according to some standard of behaviour.

Notes

1 Abraham Maslow, *Toward a Psychology of Being*, Second Edition, New York: Van Nostrand Reinhold, 1968, p. 83.

2 Margaret Mead, *Blackberry Winter: My Earlier Years*, New York: William Morrow & Company, 1972.

3 Information on the DIAL (Distance Instruction for Adult Learners) system can be obtained from The New School, 66 West 12th Street, New York, NY 10011 USA. Phone: 212-229-5880. E-mail: info@dialnsa.edu

4 Elderhostel, 75 Federal Street, Boston, MA 02110, USA.

5 Jane Burka and Lenora Yuen, *Procrastination: Why You Do It, What to Do About It*, Reading, MA: Addison-Wesley, 1983.

6 *Utne Reader*, 1624 Harmon Place, Suite 330, Minneapolis, MN 55403. Phone: 612-338-5040.

7 *Whole Earth Review*, 27 Gate Five Road, Sausalito, CA 94965. Phone: 415-332-1716.

8 An excellent book on the subject of intuition is Philip Goldberg's *The Intuitive Edge: Understanding Intuition and Applying It in Everyday Life*, Los Angeles: Jeremy P. Tarcher, 1983.

9 Connie Podesta, *Self-Esteem and the Six-Second Secret*, Newbury Park, CA: Corwin Press, 1992. (Corwin Press, Inc., A Sage Publications Company, 2455 Teller Road, Newbury Park, CA 91320, USA.)

10 For example: Matthew McKay, Ph.D., and Patrick Fanning, *Self Esteem: The Ultimate Program for Self-help*, New York: MJF Books, 1987.

11 Ken Wilber, *Grace and Grit: Spirituality and Healing in the Life and Death of Treya Killam Wilber*, Boston: Shambhala Publications, Inc., 1991.

12 Stephen Levine, *Healing into Life and Death*, New York: Anchor/Doubleday, 1989.

13 From Henry David Thoreau's *Walden*, chapter XVII

14 From Henry David Thoreau's *Journal*, June 22, 1853

15 Lines from Walt Whitman's poem "Miracles."

16 Robert Weisberg, *Creativity: Beyond the Myth of Genius*, New York: W. H. Freeman and Company, 1993.

17 Graham Wallas, *The Art of Thought*, New York: Harcourt Brace, 1926.

18 Howard Gardner, *Creating Minds: An Anatomy of Creativity Seen Through the Lives of Freud, Einstein, Picasso, Stravinsky, Eliot, Graham, and Gandhi*, New York: Basic Books, 1993.

19 More on that subject in: Copthorne Macdonald, *Toward Wisdom: Finding Our Way to Inner Peace, Love & Happiness*, Toronto: Hounslow Press, 1993.

20 As quoted in John Bartlett, *Familiar Quotations*, Fourteenth Edition, Boston: Little, Brown and Company, 1968, p. 1024.

21 Chogyam Trungpa said a lot about this problem in *Cutting Through Spiritual Materialism*, Boulder, CO: Shambhala Publications, 1973. Eric Fromm addressed it in *To Have or to Be?*, New York: Harper and Row, 1976.

22 Those readers who would like to develop this sort of mental attitude but need more information on how to go about it might find another book of mine helpful: Copthorne Macdonald, *Toward Wisdom: Finding Our Way to Inner Peace, Love & Happiness*, Toronto: Hounslow Press, 1993.

COPTHORNE MACDONALD
is available to lead workshops that focus on crafting exceptional lives for
ourselves, wisdom, and related topics. For information, contact:

WISDOM PROGRAMS
P.O. Box 2941
Charlottetown, P.E.I.
Canada C1A 8C5

Phone: (902) 894-5236
Internet: cop@cop.com